# SpringerBriefs in Business

More information about this series at http://www.springer.com/series/8860

Sebastian Văduva · Victor T. Alistar
Andrew R. Thomas · Ioan S. Fotea
Călin D. Lupiţu · Daniel S. Neagoie
Adrian F. Cioară

# Integrity in the Business Panorama

Models of European Best-Practices

Springer

Sebastian Văduva
Griffiths School of Management
Emanuel University of Oradea
Oradea
Romania

Victor T. Alistar
Transparency International Romania
Bucharest
Romania

Andrew R. Thomas
University of Akron
Akron, OH
USA

Ioan S. Fotea
Griffiths School of Management
Emanuel University of Oradea
Oradea
Romania

Călin D. Lupiţu
Emanuel University of Oradea
Oradea
Romania

Daniel S. Neagoie
Griffiths School of Management
Emanuel University of Oradea
Oradea
Romania

Adrian F. Cioară
Griffiths School of Management
Emanuel University of Oradea
Oradea
Romania

ISSN 2191-5482　　　　　　　ISSN 2191-5490　(electronic)
SpringerBriefs in Business
ISBN 978-3-319-33842-2　　　ISBN 978-3-319-33843-9　(eBook)
DOI 10.1007/978-3-319-33843-9

Library of Congress Control Number: 2016939370

© The Author(s) 2016
This work is subject to copyright. All rights are reserved by the Publisher, whether the whole or part of the material is concerned, specifically the rights of translation, reprinting, reuse of illustrations, recitation, broadcasting, reproduction on microfilms or in any other physical way, and transmission or information storage and retrieval, electronic adaptation, computer software, or by similar or dissimilar methodology now known or hereafter developed.
The use of general descriptive names, registered names, trademarks, service marks, etc. in this publication does not imply, even in the absence of a specific statement, that such names are exempt from the relevant protective laws and regulations and therefore free for general use.
The publisher, the authors and the editors are safe to assume that the advice and information in this book are believed to be true and accurate at the date of publication. Neither the publisher nor the authors or the editors give a warranty, express or implied, with respect to the material contained herein or for any errors or omissions that may have been made.

Printed on acid-free paper

This Springer imprint is published by Springer Nature
The registered company is Springer International Publishing AG Switzerland

# Contents

| | | |
|---|---|---|
| **1** | **Introduction**................................................... | 1 |
| | Sebastian Văduva and Andrew R. Thomas | |
| **2** | **Defining the Term** *Integrity*.................................... | 5 |
| | Victor T. Alistar | |
| **3** | **Activities and Risk Areas that Discredit Integrity**................. | 7 |
| | Victor T. Alistar | |
| | 3.1 Corruption ............................................. | 7 |
| | 3.2 Conflicts of Interests.................................... | 9 |
| | 3.3 Public Procurement Process............................. | 10 |
| | 3.4 Lobbying .............................................. | 10 |
| | 3.5 Political Parties' Financing/Public Donations .............. | 11 |
| | 3.6 Facilitating Payments................................... | 12 |
| | 3.7 Gifts and Donations .................................... | 13 |
| | 3.8 Discrimination ......................................... | 13 |
| | 3.9 Favoritism, Nepotism, and Political Favoritism............. | 14 |
| **4** | **Domains Where Business Integrity Matters**....................... | 15 |
| | Ioan S. Fotea and Daniel S. Neagoie | |
| | 4.1 Internal Financial/Administrative Activities Within the Organization (Internal Integrity) ........................ | 17 |
| |     4.1.1 Building Trust with Key Financial Stakeholders ......... | 18 |
| |     4.1.2 Ensuring Integrity Through Internal Control Systems..... | 18 |
| | 4.2 Integrity in the Relationships with Suppliers................... | 19 |
| |     4.2.1 Building Relationships Based on Trust with Suppliers, Through Integrity ................................ | 20 |
| |     4.2.2 Ensuring Suppliers' Integrity ....................... | 20 |
| |     4.2.3 Supply Ethics ..................................... | 21 |
| | 4.3 Integrity in Work Relationships ............................ | 21 |
| |     4.3.1 The Key Role of Employees in Building Integrity in the Business Environment ...................... | 22 |
| |     4.3.2 Fair Treatment and Procedures...................... | 22 |

|   |   | 4.3.3 | Employees' Participation and Involvement | 24 |
|---|---|---|---|---|
|   |   | 4.3.4 | Employee Privacy | 25 |
|   |   | 4.3.5 | Freedom of Expression and Conscience | 26 |
|   |   | 4.3.6 | General Presentation | 26 |
|   | 4.4 | Integrity in Recruiting Workforce | | 27 |
|   | 4.5 | Integrity in the Relationship with the Clients | | 27 |
|   |   | 4.5.1 | The Importance of Integrity in Business–Client Relationships | 28 |
|   |   | 4.5.2 | Ethical Practices in Marketing Strategy | 28 |
|   |   | 4.5.3 | Integrity in the Product Area | 29 |
|   |   | 4.5.4 | Marketing, Communication and Publicity Practices | 29 |
|   |   | 4.5.5 | Integrity in Pricing | 30 |
|   | 4.6 | Integrity in the Relationship with the Government and Public Officials | | 31 |
|   |   | 4.6.1 | The Democratic Legitimacy of the State | 31 |
|   |   | 4.6.2 | The Government's Role | 32 |
|   |   | 4.6.3 | The Importance of Integrity in the Business-Government Relationship | 32 |
|   |   | 4.6.4 | Social Capital | 33 |
|   | 4.7 | Integrity in Partnerships | | 34 |
|   |   | 4.7.1 | The Increasing Importance of Partnerships in the Business Environment | 35 |
|   |   | 4.7.2 | Integrity as a Fundamental Component for Cultivating Trust Within Partnerships | 36 |
| 5 | **The European Normative Framework for Business Ethics** | | | **39** |
|   | Sebastian Văduva and Călin D. Lupițu | | | |
|   | 5.1 | The EU Legislation | | 40 |
|   |   | 5.1.1 | Community Acquis | 40 |
|   |   | 5.1.2 | Competition Law | 41 |
|   |   | 5.1.3 | Company Law in Europe | 42 |
|   |   | 5.1.4 | Environment Law | 44 |
|   |   | 5.1.5 | Consumer Protection Law | 46 |
|   |   | 5.1.6 | Labor Law | 48 |
|   |   | 5.1.7 | Anticorruption Legislation in the EU | 49 |
|   |   | 5.1.8 | Legislation on Public Procurement | 51 |
|   |   | 5.1.9 | Legal Instruments Which Target Lobbying | 52 |
| 6 | **Developing Practice Codes for Integrity in Business** | | | **55** |
|   | Victor T. Alistar and Daniel S. Neagoie | | | |
|   | 6.1 | The Content of such Practice Codes | | 59 |
|   |   | 6.1.1 | The Content of Value Statements and Corporate Principles | 60 |
|   |   | 6.1.2 | The Content of Ethical Codes | 60 |
|   | 6.2 | Communicating Practice Codes to the Personnel and Stakeholders | | 62 |
|   |   | 6.2.1 | The Management's Role in Communicating the Code | 62 |

## 7 Practice Codes for Integrity in Business—Case Studies .......... 67
Adrian F. Cioară
7.1 Starbuck Standard's Business Conduct ...................... 67
7.2 The Nike, Inc. Conduct Code.............................. 69
7.3 The PSEG Standards on Business Integrity .................. 70

## 8 Corporate Social Responsibility—From Concept to Business Strategy ........................................... 73
Sebastian Văduva and Daniel S. Neagoie
8.1 The Government as a Facilitator .......................... 76
    8.1.1 The European Standards and Guidelines ............... 76
    8.1.2 Promoting CSR in the European Member States ......... 77
8.2 Case Study: Sweden...................................... 81
    8.2.1 The Understanding of CSR ......................... 81
    8.2.2 National Strategies ................................ 81
    8.2.3 Visibility......................................... 82
    8.2.4 Transparency and Reporting......................... 82
    8.2.5 The Financial Sector............................... 83
    8.2.6 The Public Procurement Process ..................... 83
    8.2.7 CSR and SMEs.................................... 84
    8.2.8 The Activities of Companies Outside State Borders ...... 84
8.3 Case Study: Great Britain................................. 85
    8.3.1 The Understanding of CSR ......................... 85
    8.3.2 National Strategies ................................ 86
    8.3.3 A CSR Source: Great Britain's Department of Trade and Industry .............................. 86
    8.3.4 The Activities of the Other Ministers.................. 86
    8.3.5 Compulsory Report ............................... 87
    8.3.6 Visibility......................................... 87
    8.3.7 Transparency and Reporting......................... 88
    8.3.8 The Financial Sector............................... 88
    8.3.9 Public Procurement ............................... 89
    8.3.10 Business Activities Outside Great Britain .............. 89
8.4 Case Study: France....................................... 89
    8.4.1 The Understanding of CSR in France ................. 90
    8.4.2 The National Strategy.............................. 90
    8.4.3 Visibility......................................... 91
    8.4.4 Transparency and Reporting......................... 91
    8.4.5 Criticisms for the System's Efficiency in General ........ 92
    8.4.6 The Financial Sector............................... 92
    8.4.7 Public Procurement ............................... 93
    8.4.8 The Activities of Companies Outside France's Borders .... 93
8.5 Solutions for Implementing CSR Strategies ................... 94
    8.5.1 Conduct Codes for CSR............................ 94
    8.5.2 Suggestion of Models for the Corporate Conduct Codes.... 94
    8.5.3 The Content of Conduct Codes for CSR ............... 95

|  |  | 8.5.4 | Implementing Conduct Codes | 96 |
|---|---|---|---|---|
|  |  | 8.5.5 | Monitoring Progress | 97 |
|  |  | 8.5.6 | Responsible Accounting for Society and Environment | 97 |

## 9 Models of Good Practices ... 99
Călin D. Lupiţu and Adrian F. Cioară

    9.1   Case Study: Anglo-American PLC ... 99
          9.1.1   CSR Vision ... 100
          9.1.2   Strategic Orientation ... 100
          9.1.3   CSR Initiatives ... 101
          9.1.4   Independent Evaluation ... 103
    9.2   Case Study: Danone S.A. ... 104
          9.2.1   CSR Vision ... 105
          9.2.2   Strategic Orientation ... 105
          9.2.3   CSR Initiatives ... 106
          9.2.4   Independent Evaluation ... 109
    9.3   Case Study: Bayer ... 110
          9.3.1   CSR Vision ... 110
          9.3.2   Strategic Orientation ... 111
          9.3.3   CSR Initiatives ... 111
          9.3.4   Independent Evaluations ... 114
    9.4   Case Study: Santander ... 116
          9.4.1   CSR Vision ... 117
          9.4.2   Strategic Orientation ... 117
          9.4.3   CSR Initiatives ... 118
          9.4.4   Independent Evaluations ... 120

**Conclusions** ... 123

**Recommendations** ... 125

**References** ... 127

# Chapter 1
# Introduction

**Sebastian Văduva and Andrew R. Thomas**

The global financial crisis represented an alarm signal regarding the need for solid principles to guide conduct throughout the entire business world, and especially in Europe. Trust in the free market and in businesses has diminished and, as a consequence of the crisis, politicians and the civil society have asked for greater control and a regularization of business practices. The exclusive pursuit of one's own interest and of profit maximizing by any means, together with business integrity breaches, were considered the foundation stones upon which the crisis was built. It was even suggested that *"the global financial crisis might be a case-study example of integrity—or of the lack thereof, rather"*.[1] Demand for a business conduct of integrity and for high ethical standards has increased significantly as a consequence of the economic crisis; still, both concepts have already long been part of the business world's vocabulary. Integrity has been the most frequently mentioned concept in the companies'[2] mission and values statements and it is *"the trait most often quoted"* by the business community.

Integrity nevertheless remains a relatively fuzzy concept for both society and the business community itself, which has started to increasingly perceive integrity as being a corporate exercise in PR. This simplistic approach has led to integrity

---

[1]Ref. [16].
[2]Ref. [34].

S. Văduva (✉)
Griffiths School of Management, Emanuel University of Oradea,
Oradea, Romania
e-mail: sebastianvaduva@emanuel.ro

A.R. Thomas
University of Akron, Akron, OH, USA
e-mail: art@uakron.edu

breaches that propelled activities devastating to the political, social, and economic environment. In a society with an ever-developing, competitive, and diversified business environment, integrity is crucial for long-term success and must be placed at the center of any business strategy.

Integrity breaches generate unethical and illegal business practices, with a devastating effect on the political, social, and economic spheres of society. While corruption is strongly linked to the notion of integrity, business integrity includes more than the prevention of corrupt activities. Integrity involves cultivating moral imagination when it has to deal with everyday unethical practices. When integrity is absent, these unethical and illegal practices infiltrate society and generate a spiral of resent, cynicism, and negativism.

From a business point of view, these activities occur during daily interactions with the key stakeholders. Building trust-based relationships is crucial to ensuring the success of a business. Without trusting a business' integrity, transaction costs increase and the economic environment shrinks. The global financial crisis provides a pure example of what happens when trust and safety within the business environment are lost. Integrity breaches build the foundation for illegal unethical practices growing in business relations. Integrity in business relations is a key component of the long-term success of a certain business or society.

While obeying the law is essential in building business integrity, integrity is a much broader concept than obeying the law. Laws are vast and cannot offer guidance for the daily ethical dilemmas that the business environment faces. Integrity includes the ability of being consistent with one's moral values and principles and places society's wishes at the center of business decision-making. Businesses have to have a high sense of social accountability. The cornerstone upon which a culture of integrity is built within a certain business is the ethics code. It explicitly states the values and principles a company adheres to. The continuous promotion, support, and communication of its stipulations provide the basis upon which integrity in business is built.

Research showed that a company's ethical behavior in its relationship with its stakeholders has the potential of improving competitiveness by creating common values. The improvement registered from a company competitiveness standpoint is largely related to the strong position a responsible company holds in relation to consumers' trust and its long-term sustainability.

The argument in favor of CSR incorporates the success registered by many companies in attaining high performances on the market as a result of their ethical conduct. The benefits brought to society in general, thanks to business integrity in particular, are clear, and the promoting of CSR by governmental structures is analyzed in order for it to reveal its potential as an alternative to the restrictive norms, thus offering more room for innovations and the improvement of social and environmental policies' efficiency.

Governments must enable and encourage companies to adopt their own CSR strategies, which have the advantage of generating the voluntary commitment to integrity pacts, which otherwise adopted would be too rigid and hard to implement.

Thus, an efficient CSR must be elaborated in accordance with the company's operations themselves. CSR is viewed as a strategic instrument used to reach a company's business targets in a way in which the company also creates common values for the society in general. In order to achieve this, it is necessary that the CSR policy is directly linked to the company's fundamental operations that have been strategically developed to increase corporative value. The approached case studies prove that there is no single public CSR policy beneficial for everyone (*one size fits all*), but a viable strategy must emerge from within the company.

# Chapter 2
# Defining the Term *Integrity*

**Victor T. Alistar**

In the field of ethics in business, integrity is the most wanted trait the business environment aspires to. It occupies a central place in the value statements and ethics codes of many companies and it is a trait which companies are willing to present to the stakeholders both within and beyond the company. Still, integrity is often improperly defined. It is important that all facets of integrity be investigated in order to understand why it is fundamental to the daily challenges of the business environment. Moreover, integrity is seen as an essential component in the long-term building of successful business relations. Etymologically speaking, the word *integrity* draws its roots from the Latin word *integritatem*, which means *totality* or *fulness*. It is the quality of being "a whole," or "*uncorrupted*". Integrity can be defined as a moral principle. Conceptualizing integrity includes it as a moral trait. A person of integrity has developed and has adhered to a strict moral code which includes multiple virtues such as honesty, bravery, and sincerity. These moral virtues are the cornerstones of human interactions; moreover, these virtues are acquired and developed through human interaction. Society depends on human interactions in order to satisfy needs and this is conferred by the understanding of the term of reciprocity. Reciprocity means treating the others with respect and kindness in order for us to receive the same respect and kindness.

Integrity is not only a personal, but also a "*social virtue*".[1] A person of integrity will act not only by the coherence of their values and moral convictions. Such a person is aware and mindful of society's needs when making a decision. Qualities

---

[1]Ref. [4].

V.T. Alistar (✉)
Transparency International Romania, Bucharest, Romania
e-mail: victor.alistar@transparency.org.ro

such as bravery, receptiveness, loyalty, and compassion allow a person to keep their integrity when facing social obstacles that might have adverse effects on their living standards. Koehn shows that, overall, integrity means more than the coherence of commitments and actions, even of the moral ones. Integrity means compassion and raising social awareness to *"self-wholeness"*.[2]

---

[2]Ref. [9].

# Chapter 3
# Activities and Risk Areas that Discredit Integrity

Victor T. Alistar

Integrity in business is intimately linked with battling corruption. While business integrity involves more than avoiding corrupt activities, a considerable part of the literature and the legislation regarding business integrity is focused on corruption. A business that places integrity at its center is less susceptible to develop any corrupt activities. Actions in the business area give rise to complex ethical dilemmas. The gifts and donations area is such an example. Giving and receiving gifts has always played an important part in facilitating business relations. It is important to understand what constitutes a gift and what constitutes bribery, in order to avoid accusations of illegal or unethical activities. Moreover, an interdiction regarding offering gifts can lead to accusations of lack of integrity. Consequently, corruption and unethical behaviors erode social morality, introducing long-term additional costs for the business and an insecure economic environment within the country.

## 3.1 Corruption

Transparency International defines corruption as being *the abuse of entrusted power for private gain.*[1] This is a broad definition which includes the notion of obtaining pecuniary advantages by breaking official attributions and the rights of others.

Corruption may be further classified as main, petty and, dependent on the money sum involved and the sector it is signaled in.

---

[1]Transparency International, http://www.transparency.org/.

V.T. Alistar (✉)
Transparency International Romania, Bucharest, Romania
e-mail: victor.alistar@transparency.org.ro

© The Author(s) 2016
S. Văduva et al., *Integrity in the Business Panorama*,
SpringerBriefs in Business, DOI 10.1007/978-3-319-33843-9_3

- **Main corruption**: it is comprised of the corruption deeds of high-level representatives of the business and governmental environment, who distort policies and the central functioning of the state, allowing its leaders to obtain personal gains at the expense of the public good.
- **Petty corruption**: this form of corruption refers to daily abuses perpetrated by public officials of low and medium level in their interactions with citizens, which most often take the form of obtaining basic goods or services such as health, education, and may include legal organisms or other institutions.
- **Political corruption**: it refers to manipulating policies, institutions and procedures or regulations in allocating resources and financing by power holders, who abuse their position in support of their power and status.

**The World Bank** has identified corruption as being the sole greatest obstacle that economic and social development has to face.[2] From a political point of view, corruption acts in order to alter democracy and the rule of law. Democratic institutions lose their legitimacy when they are abusively used for personal interests. Corruption leads to the distortion of the free market and competition structures which repress economic development and discourage investments. The rare investments of public resources are made into projects that benefit private interests to the detriment of the public good and lead to collective costs for all the members of the society. Corrupt activities lead to the unrestricted destruction of the environment under the given circumstances in which companies all over the world bribe in order to obtain free but condemnable work practices. The estimated financial costs of corruption show the following[3]:

- The cost of corruption globally equals more than 5 % of GDP per capita.
- Corruption adds a 10 % cost to conducting businesses at a global level and up to 25 % in public acquisition contracts in some developing countries.
- Businesses that take into consideration relocating from a country with a low corruption level to a country with a medium or high level of corruption must take into account estimating a 20 % fee for foreign businesses as a result of increased corruption.
- In the European Union, the general estimated cost of corruption is of approximately €120 billion per year, although the results of a recent study conducted by the Hertie School of Governance in Berlin has shown the real cost of corruption to be of €323 billion per year.[4]

Moreover, corruption can be classified as being isolated or systemic. Isolated corruption emerges where non-corrupt activities are normal. The actors of the public and private sectors support integrity and the non-corrupt balance is easily implemented. Systemic or omnipresent corruption emerges where corruption is part of

---

[2]The World Bank, http://www.worldbank.org/.
[3]International Chamber of Commerce, *The Trial of Businesses against Corruption*.
[4]Ref. [31].

the routine of everyday activities.[5] It leads to a warping of material incentives and to *a psychology of defensiveness and cynicism.*[6] This psychology determines non-financial costs. It corrodes the fabric of society. Corrupt activities lead to disbelief in the democratic system and the rule of law. It can act as a stimulant of negative behaviors in the social and daily business relationships.

## 3.2 Conflicts of Interests

Transparency International defines conflicts of interests as being *situations where an individual or an entity they work for, whether the government, the business environment, the media or the organizations of the civil society, has to choose between the obligations and requirements of their job and those of their own interests.*[7]

The conflict of interests is different from corruption: *in reality, the conflict of interests is understood as being a situation, not an action, and it is obvious that a public person can find themselves in a position of conflict of interests without actually being corrupt.*[8]

Conflicts of interests can be classified as being with or without pecuniary interests:

- **Pecuniary interests**: refer to monetary transactions. They are linked to the potential financial gains or losses, for instance the rise of land or property value. It can also lead to financial benefits for family members, friends or business partners.
- **No pecuniary interests**: these are linked to benefits that are not of a monetary or financial nature. An example of that is hiring one's own relatives on certain positions within their company.

Conflicts of interest may be classified as being real, perceived and potential.

- **Real conflicts of interests**: one's own interests interfere with one's duties and responsibilities.
- **Perceived conflicts of interests**: the perception that one's own interests may have an inappropriate influence on workplace attributions.
- **Potential conflicts of interests**: the situations where the personal interests of an employee may overlap with their work attributions in the future.

---

[5]Ref. [48].

[6]Klitgaard, R., *Tackling Corruption in Haiti,* Claremont Graduate University, Claremont, CA, 2010.

[7]Ref. [13].

[8]Ref. [38].

While a person may find themselves in a conflict of interests situation without being corrupt, one must acknowledge the fact that corruption often appears where personal interests have inappropriately influenced individual performances. Due to this particular reason, it is crucial to prevent and manage conflicts of interests, as part of broader initiatives for preventing and fighting corruption.[9]

## 3.3 Public Procurement Process

Transparency International considers public procurement the favorable environment where the large-scale corruption takes place, with highlights on the defense, construction and petroleum sectors, where the majority of high-corruption practices occur.

The World Bank has estimated that approximately $1.5 thousand billion result from conferring public contracts that are usually influenced by corruption and it has been estimated that the volume of bribe in public procurement alone amounts to $200 billion per year.[10] There are certain factors that determine corruption in the public procurement procedures:

- Cartel practices
- High-ranked people in the business environment and in government can warp the public procurement domain, for instance, by increasing regulations in order to optimize corruption gains. The same result can be obtained by bribing public officials to modify regulations in favor of third parties, using contracts without auctions, or with just one bidder (sole source)
- There are also legal means, such as lobbying, used to influence the business environment for the benefit of private contractors.

Corruption in the public procurement system leads to higher costs of services for the citizens of a certain state.

## 3.4 Lobbying

OECD [33] defines **lobbying** as being: *the written or oral communication with a public official to influence legislation, policy or administrative decisions, often focuses on the legislative branch at the national and sub-national levels. However, it also takes place in the executive branch, for example, to influence the adoption of regulations or the design of projects and contracts. Consequently, the term*

---

[9]Ref. [32].
[10]Ref. [22].

*public officials includes civil and public servants, employees and holders of public office in the executive and legislative branches, whether elected or appointed.*[11]

This attempt to influence a legislative, public policy, or administrative decision can take the form of an informal and/or persuasive regulation.[12] McGrath (2000),[13] quoted by Crane and Matten [7],[14] distinguishes between the different types of lobbying:

- **Establishing the setting**: employed in essence in order to increase awareness of problems the industry has and to create a setting where future influences may be introduced.
- **Monitoring**: this aim of lobbying allows for governmental information regarding legislative aspects, or those regulation aspects which can affect the industry, to be received in advance.
- **Provision of information by political decision-makers**: when policies are being drafted, governmental officials request information from the business environment, information which is going to help them with their decision-making processes
- **Influencing and advocacy**: the ultimate purpose of lobbying is influencing the political decision-makers, by providing them with politics-oriented expertise
- **Applying pressure**: used to persuade the taking of action one way or another; the pressure can involve direct or indirect *warnings* concerning the possible consequences of certain policies.

OECD[15] admits to the necessity and importance of lobbying in the democratic society. Still, the negative effects lobbying has in undermining the legitimacy of democracy through its lack of transparency cannot be neglected. Transparency International [46][16] believes lobbying can be perceived as potential *legal corruption* due to its opaque rules and to the lack of process transparency.

## 3.5 Political Parties' Financing/Public Donations

In the Global Corruption Report (2004), Transparency International defines **political corruption** as *the abuse of entrusted power by political leaders for private gain.*

This involves not only pecuniary aspects, but it can also take the form of *influence peddling* and offering favors. The legitimacy of public donations can be questioned, although in most European countries divulging such payments is

---

[11]Ref. [33].
[12]Ref. [7].
[13]McGrath [30].
[14]Ref. [7].
[15]OECD, *Private Interests, Public Conduct: The Essence of Lobbying*, OECD.
[16]Ref. [46].

mandatory. These payments can lead to aspects concerning conflicts of interests. Moreover, public donations can affect a company's image and lead to potential questionable behavior on behalf of the employees.[17] The Global Corruption report cites the Worldwide Economic study (2003), which has discovered that in 89 % out of the 102 questioned countries it is believed that legal political donations have an effect ranging from moderate to high in influencing certain political decisions. The perception of such kinds of payments can lead to a downward spiral of mistrust in the business environment and the political institutions of the state.

## 3.6 Facilitating Payments

**Facilitating payments** are payments made to a public official with the purpose of accelerating a business transaction or an administrative process.

In the legal system of many states, facilitating payments is a different concept to bribery. Many companies take advantage of this distinction when using these payments. The American Corrupt Practices and Anti-Bribe Provisions Act allow this distinction and stipulates that *there is an exception in banning bribery for facilitating or accelerating the performance of routine governmental activities*. The Bribery Act of 2010 (The United Kingdom), on the other hand, does not allow any exceptions regarding facilitating payments. The Serious Fraud Office Executive and the leader of the Public Office have published procedural guides concerning this document, which show there is no exception in facilitating payments, therefore any such payments will be considered an instance of breaking the Bribery Act. The distinction between what is considered facilitating payments and bribery has become unclear. Zero tolerance regarding this policy should be introduced for the following reasons:

- These payments can have an eroding effect on the ethical climate of an organization and can affect the ability to instate policies, which leads to more corrupt practices
- They lead to harmful perceptions of the employees of a company, who feel that business integrity and antifraud policies are not equally applied
- Using the evidence of facilitating payments made by a company can have a harmful effect upon its image
- The real difficulty of making the difference between what constitutes bribery and what constitutes facilitating payments. This practice can lead to the possibility that a company may find itself on a slippery slope to utilizing direct corrupt practices
- The organization's stakeholders' perception regarding business integrity is deteriorating and can lead to a climate of mistrust

---

[17]Ref. [7].

## 3.7 Gifts and Donations

**Gift offering** is an area that needs to be carefully managed in the business environment. The ethics around gift offering and receiving can be complex and attention must be paid to such areas as cultural sensitivity and good industry practices.

Gift offering and receiving has always played an important role in facilitating business relations. Still, the line between what constitutes a gift and what constitutes bribery can be unclear and may lead an organization to unethical or even illegal behavior practices.

**Bribery Act (2010)** offers insight on what differentiates a gift from bribe. Gifts can be considered bribery if they have *the intention of inducing an inappropriate behavior*. The timing of the gift is also relevant. If the gift is offered a short time after, before or during a business transaction, such as an auction, it can be interpreted as being inadequate or even constituting bribery. To insure the highest integrity levels in a business, a company must have a clear understanding of the inherent dangers of offering and receiving gifts. Another aspect of integrity is that the situational context must be taken into account when a decision that has the potential of undermining the integrity is made. Timing awareness and cultural sensitivity is extremely important in making decisions regarding offering gifts in order to maintain integrity.

## 3.8 Discrimination

**Discrimination** can be defined as being *the differential treatment of certain individuals or groups based on abusive classification criteria.*[18] The common bases of discrimination are gender, age, religious orientation, and sexual orientation.

In the working environment, discrimination takes place when employees face differentiated treatments that have nothing to do with workplace performance or qualifications. Furthermore, this can be grouped as direct and indirect discrimination. Direct discrimination happens when an individual or a group of individuals are being unfairly treated relative to one of the reasons for discrimination. Indirect discrimination, as per its definition in the EU directives, appears *where a provision, criterion or practice which is apparently neutral has a damaging effect on people with* a certain ethical or racial origin or religion, disability or sexual orientation, placing them in a disadvantageous position compared to other people.

---

[18]Eurofound, www.eurofound.europa.eu.

## 3.9 Favoritism, Nepotism, and Political Favoritism

**Favoritism** involves the preferential treatment of a person based on criteria that are not related to his or her ability to fulfill their duties but, for instance, have to do with their affiliation to certain groups or organizations. The clientele is linked to favoritism in the sense that it involves granting public offices to persons that have helped in the election of the ones now in power, so the latter would appoint them to public offices. **Political favoritism** has a stricter definition, in the sense that it refers to granting favors to friends and associates. **Nepotism** means granting favors to relatives, regardless of their merits.

Promoting integrity operates as an agent for combating illegal and unethical practices. As shown in the study this far, these activities charge enormous taxes from the social, economic, and political environment of a state. Integrity is a key component in building trust within business relationships. In the absence of integrity, the illegal and unethical practices rise and endanger the long-term success of a company.

# Chapter 4
# Domains Where Business Integrity Matters

**Ioan S. Fotea and Daniel S. Neagoie**

Building business relationships based on trust is essential in obtaining long-term success. The notion of trust is closely knit with the one of integrity. Moreover, promoting trust in a relationship where lack of integrity is perceived becomes impossible. A facet of integrity is that of acting with consistency and in depth, while being aware of the situations from the surrounding environment. This is fundamental in building business relationships based on trust, where decision-making is perceived as being consistent, with lofty moral ideals and ethical conduct. Developing an atmosphere based on trust within business relationships is absolutely necessary for the global business environment. Moreover, good faith and trust are essential traits for the business environment. *Without trust, business as we know it is impossible.*[1] Thus, *from a sociological, psychological, and economic perspective, there are solid justifications regarding the need for integrity in business and in the current continuously changing business context.*

(i) **The Sociological Perspective of Trust**
One of the most important aspects of decision-making is linked to its orientation toward the future. When the actors predict with practical certainty the result of a future happening, there is no need for trust anymore. Trust in the result is secured. Still, social actors can predict the future with a percentage of probability which

---

[1]Ref. [1].

---

I.S. Fotea (✉)
Griffiths School of Management, Emanuel University of Oradea, Oradea, Romania
e-mail: ioan.fotea@emanuel.ro

D.S. Neagoie
Griffiths School of Management, Emanuel University of Oradea, Oradea, Romania
e-mail: daniel.neagoie@emanuel.ro

leaves room for uncertainty. Moreover, certain situations attest to the fact that the actors cannot even make these predictions probable. Trust becomes crucial in these situations. Without trust, the social actors will have to take into considerations all the unpredictable situations, which will lead to a block in decision-making due to their arbitrariness.[2] Although trust absorbs uncertainty and diminishes complications, it also produces risks. A risk is that the donors will have as their purpose diminishing their own risk when they decide to place their trust in another social actor. If the actors cannot find a good hypothesis that the risk is minor, they could easily revoke the partnerships.[3] Perceiving a lack of integrity will exponentially increase the risk and will create an antithesis to building strong businesses and social relationships.

(ii) **The psychological perspective of trust**
Trust is defined as being *the will of the person who grants the trust of being vulnerable to the actions of the person being granted the trust, in hopes that the latter will act by means of a certain conduct.* On the other hand, the honesty of the person being granted the trust depends on three characteristics: capacity, goodwill and integrity. Then it is decided whether to place the trust in someone or not, the person offering the trust will weigh all these characteristics in order to decide if the mentioned person is trustworthy. Perceiving a lack of integrity will lead in a business setting, from the point of view of the person offering the trust, to perceiving the business as being frivolous; moreover, it can influence the person offering the trust so as not to be in contact with that business. The tendency to offer trust depends on pervious experiences and dispositional factors, such as personality.[4] A business that is perceived as having a poor history and unethical practices will reduce the tendency of the person giving the trust to place the trust in that person. Psychology literature argues that trust, too, is progressively won; still, it can be immediately destroyed. Once trust is lost, it costs and takes a long while to be built back. This principle reflects a fundamental mechanism of human psychology, known as the principle of asymmetry. According to this principle, distrust is not necessarily the opposite of trust. There are different ways in which this is learned and they function differently. The principle of asymmetry provides an important lesson that states that lack of integrity can have long-term effects in business relations, which can take years of work to be remedied.

(iii) **The economic perspective of trust**
Adam Smith's theory requires integrating trust in the marketplace system, in order to allow the actors to participate to it with a certain degree of certainty. Without trusting the integrity of the people in the system, transaction costs will be too high

---

[2]Ref. [44].

[3]Bachmann, R., *Trust, Power and Control in Trans-Organizational Relations,* Organization Studies (Walter de Gruyter GmbH & Co. KG).

[4]Ref. [29].

and the marketplace system will fail. When trust in the marketplace is low, transactional costs rise due to the perceived high risk level. It is unlikely then that the individuals take place in economic operations and thus the market shrinks. Also, when trust increases and the market is stimulated, the energy and creativity of the economic actors leads toward high levels of transactions, thus expanding the market. The perceptions of integrity of the main economic actors in the marketplace system are essential for ensuring the market's vitality and raising the welfare of that society. Economy literature offers, in addition, the proof that a society based on a high trust level (high-trust) has higher economic performances than societies based on a low trust level (low-trust). Zak and Knack show that *a sufficiently high trust level is crucial for successful development.*[5] Game theory of advances the concept of the prisoner's dilemma, which is the canon example of the Nash balance. In an uncooperative scheme of a single-shot game (one-shot), the parties find themselves in a state of balance (the Nash balance) through which neither party modifies their strategy. In fact, there is a strong deterrent against modifying the strategy. The optimal Pareto state exists; however, without cooperation this state will be unrealizable. Many game studies pointed out a conflict around this theory. In high trust level societies, even without cooperation, the individuals surpass the Nash balance and the prisoner's dilemma. In this kind of societies, perceptions toward integrity and reciprocity increase the level of trust which then significantly influences growth rates.[6]

From these three perspectives, it becomes obvious that integrity in business is essential when building relationships based on trust, which ultimately determine a successful business future. Key business relationships include those with the stakeholders and the creditors of the organization, the relationships with suppliers, work relationships, the relationship with the government and society, and the relationships in the business environment.

## 4.1 Internal Financial/Administrative Activities Within the Organization (Internal Integrity)

The financial function within a business has a fundamental responsibility in generating the necessary funds to make sure the business runs properly. Moreover, this function must invest in these funds in a way which maximizes shareholder value. Success in business is based on the quality of these decisions and on the perceptions of the key actors toward financial and administrative activities' integrity.

---

[5]Ref. [49].
[6]*Ibid.*

### 4.1.1 Building Trust with Key Financial Stakeholders

Communicating with key stakeholders, such as shareholders and creditors, is based mainly on financial information by issuing financial statements. The perception of integrity regarding financial statements wins stakeholders' trust by providing them with exact data, on time and transparently. The lack of integrity in the financial statements and all administrative and economic activities of an organization can lead to total trust loss in the relationships with the stakeholders. Lack of integrity can generate higher financing costs, leading to possible legal implications and even bankruptcy.

Issuing financial statements is regulated by accounting standards and the information exposed in these statements must offer a *true and fair image* of business performance and the position at that time. The Fourth European Directive regarding the rights of trading companies established the concept of this kind of image in the community law of these companies. Still, accounting standards admit certain discretion regarding precise accounting procedures. Under these circumstances, the procedures need exercising judgment on the businesses' part. Moreover, subjectivity in interpreting quality standards can lead to aggressive and inadequate financial reporting standards. The factors that could lead to such practices may include, but are not limited to, the following: *different economic environments, pressures in execution or managing, or remuneration incentives connected to short-term objectives.*

In order to ensure the financial statements' integrity and to maintain trust in key business relationships, those involved in the process of statement issuing are required to have a high level of integrity. Still, financial and administrative activities in a society should be monitored by a robust internal control system that supervised the making of these financial statements. The internal control system is crucial in steering and managing risks within the financial activities of the company. The system will play a key role in ensuring transparency and responsibility, which will contribute to creating a culture of integrity in business.

### 4.1.2 Ensuring Integrity Through Internal Control Systems

Internal control systems offer integrity ensurance mechanisms regarding financial situations. At the same time, they offer a mechanism to secure integrity within financial activities in a business. Corruption appears where there are insufficient or inadequate control systems. Weak internal controls in fields such as financial management, audit and staff systems will act as an incentive for the circumstances of corruption activities. Weak internal control systems provide the incentives for corrupt activities due to their limited exposure risks and detection of illegal practices.[7] While personal integrity is very important in these areas, a solid

---

[7] Anti-Corruption Resource Centre, *The Basics of Anti-Corruption*, www.u4.no/articles/thebasics-of-anti-corruption/.

internal control system will provide procedures and guidance in these areas. All transactions must be recorded correctly and accurately so that financial systems can be supported. The existence of hidden accounts or obscure funds must be strictly prohibited. The internal control system provides:

- A way through which the resources of the organization are directed, monitored and measured.
- Authorizations for personnel to make certain specific transactions.
- A fraud prevention and detection mechanism.
- Policies and procedures through which transactions are registered and which allow the preparation of financial issue statements in accordance with accounting standards.
- Directive limits which give permissions and guidance regarding the use or misuse of the organization's goods.
- A system through which the use of active recordings can be overlapped with the existing real assets and with the adequate investigation procedures when differences emerge.

Financial and administrative control systems are essential in communicating policies and procedures aimed at managing any potentially emerging situations of conflicts of interests, by introducing controls in the public procurement processes and detailing related policies, such as the fundamentals of building a culture of integrity and establishing trust in relationships with the stakeholders, as these are crucial for success in the ongoing business. The integrity in business systems and anticorruption policies go farther than only discovering and penalizing corrupt practices. These systems have the purpose of preventing corruption by building transparent and responsible governing relationships that reduce incentives for corruption activities, and by the consolidation of the internal setting for ensuring business integrity.

## 4.2 Integrity in the Relationships with Suppliers

All successful companies build solid relationships with their suppliers, based on trust and respect; still, these relationships can also produce situations where business integrity is altered due to illegal or unethical practices. Many times, the contracts between the parties involve considerable amounts of money. Although it is important for the company to act with integrity in the business relationships to build trust, a supplier using unethical tactics can also unfavorably project upon the reputation of the business. In the past, companies used to state that their suppliers' practices were not their job but, due to the predominant conditions in society and the rise of the public's awareness regarding unethical practices, they must pay special attention to the business practices throughout the entire supply chain.

## 4.2.1 Building Relationships Based on Trust with Suppliers, Through Integrity

The public procurement processes of a company produce situations which lead to ethical and legal ramifications for the business. Bribery, illegal commissions, hospitality, and gifts can be offered to the personnel responsible for public procurement so as to ensure preferential treatment for the supplier's company. As employees of the firm, the purchasers must act in the best interest of the firm. The presence of material or moral conflicts can lead to situations in which the company faces lack of trust from the business' stakeholders. Perceptions of the appearance of unethical practices erode trust and consolidates a culture of dishonesty that, once implemented, can be difficult to banish. Unethical practices perpetuate an unethical behavior cycle. For this reason, the relative power of both parties in respect to the supplier-buyer relationship has been the subject of much debate in literature. While its competitive force is used for obtaining bigger profits, it must be reminded that its faulty use can affect the organization's reputation and can lead to distrustful relationships, which can cause long-run problems for the business. Besides, rigorous internal controls are essential for stopping unethical practices that can be manifested by giving bribery, offering gifts and hospitality within these relationships. Also, the business must take into consideration the effect the power abuse has on the level of trust in this relationship. The costs associated with the lack of integrity in this relationship lead to a degraded reputation, to loss of business opportunities, to deteriorated relationships, and potential legal ramifications.

## 4.2.2 Ensuring Suppliers' Integrity

On a global level, supply chains have given birth to major problems regarding the way suppliers develop their business practices. These practices can project a bad image upon supply organizations. The contestation made by the business environment saying that it, itself, is not responsible for the practices of the suppliers cannot stand especially due to the rise of the public's awareness regarding unethical practices in the business environment. Pressure groups have succeeded to draw the public's attention to a lot of the unethical work practices that had the effect of deteriorating the integrity of the mentioned firm. Some of these interest areas include: *precarious working conditions, children exploitation practices, forced work practices, equality and precarious health and security procedures and slow work environment protection practices.*

Companies are facing an extended responsibility chain through which their business has to communicate policies and procedures with their supply chain partners, with the intent to regulate and control its supplying practices.[8] This can be made possible through ethical supplying processes and checking their suppliers' books.

---

[8]Ref. [7].

## 4.2.3 Supply Ethics

Supplying from sources which maintain ethical work relationships involves including social and environment criteria in the acquisition decisions of a business. Through this supply, companies condition their supply chain partners with regard to ethical problems, from children exploitation practices to illegal acquisitions or corruption deeds. Supply from sources that maintain ethical work relationships can be defined, as a large concept, as *including some explicit ethical and/or environmental criteria in the programs, procedures and managing policies of the supply chain.*[9] Supply from resources that maintain ethical work relationships becomes an essential self-regulation mechanism for companies working in countries where legislation is weak or it is inadequately applied. The business environment can form alliances with the administrations, with non-profit organizations and regional, national or international companies in order to enforce supply standards from sources that maintain ethical work relationships. Alliances form strong coalitions in order to ensure business integrity in the supply chain. An example of an alliance which ensures ethical standards is the Ethical Exchange Initiative (EEI), which is self-labeled as *an innovative alliance of companies, trade unions and volunteering organizations.*[10] The alliance has the objective of improving employment standards within supply chains and applying the best supply practices. Supplying from sources which maintain ethical work relationships can be communicated through conduct codes; still, in order to make sure this is not seen as merely a public relations exercise, monitoring and implementing policies are necessary in order to ensure compliance. Supply from sources which maintain ethical work relationships becomes one of the main instruments in ensuring integrity within the supply chain and thus leads to protecting integrity in the business environment and also protecting reputation. Thus, as supply chains worldwide become standardized, the relationship between suppliers and businesses must be based on trust. The lack of integrity of one member of the chain or a chain with inadequate control measurements can have disastrous effects not only on the business within the chain but also on the whole industry.

## 4.3 Integrity in Work Relationships

In Europe, work relationships are based on *a fairly dense legislation network which offers legally enshrined solutions to a large number of problems between companies and employees.*[11] This legislation places the rights and obligations of both parties in the work relationship. Protections are invariably considered on the

---

[9]*Ibid.*
[10]Ethical Exchange Initiative, http://www.ethicaltrade.org/.
[11]Ref. [7].

employee's side; moreover, this legislation can be seen as a compensatory force for balancing the unequal negotiating power that companies hold in this relationship. Still, the law only provides a general setting, which leaves a considerable amount to be debated by both partners of the relationship. In order to build a culture of integrity in business, a policies-and-procedures-based setting that promotes and vitalizes legal and ethical practices in the business environment must be developed.

### 4.3.1 The Key Role of Employees in Building Integrity in the Business Environment

The employees of a company play a vital role in building and ensuring the integrity of the business environment. Through their daily actions on all the levels of the company, the culture of integrity is being shaped. This culture will allow, in addition, for the cultivation of long-run relationships based on trust with the business' key-partners. Still, establishing a culture of integrity in the business world requires more than employing people with a high level of perceived personal integrity. Difficulties in establishing these individual qualities may emerge after only a couple of meetings; moreover, people that come from different cultural backgrounds and systems may have values and beliefs that clash with those of the organization. Consequently, the organizations must create a set of policies and procedures which have as their purpose coordinating their actions. These policies and procedures must promote, vitalize and sustain the values and principles of an organization, while the policies and procedures have the purpose of establishing expected levels of behavior in an organization, since their mere existence will not develop the integrity of the business environment. Behavioral norms are developed through social interaction and reciprocity. Promoting integrity in the business environment requires that the authority does not only establish and create these policies, but it also practices the same goals. Unethical or incorrect decisions made by the executives in an organization can perpetuate in the entire company. Moreover, abusive or unethical business actions in the working relationship will lead to distrust. Integrity within the work relationship is essential for attaining integrity in the extended business environment.

### 4.3.2 Fair Treatment and Procedures

The principle of fairness is strongly rooted in integrity. An awareness and practice of the concept of fair processes and procedures is essential in building a culture of integrity within a business. The right to a fair process is rooted in the notion of procedural justice. The notion of justice can be classified as procedural, distributive, and punitive justice. The procedural one is a form which *requires applying norms and procedures in a consistent and impartial way, avoiding arbitrary decisions and without discriminating on grounds other than merit.*[12] There is the idea that equity and transparency in the decision-making processes exists, and it allocates resources and resolves disputes. In a business context, the equitable process and fair procedures are essential in cases such as promotion opportunities and disciplinary procedures. Leventhal [26], in his theory upon this kind of justice, has provided six rules.[13] These are:

- **Consistency**: principles should apply to all people across time. In what concerns the people, it dictates equality in decision-making procedures. The temporal dimension suggests that rules must be followed in every case. Any change in procedures must be communicated to the ones who are going to be affected by this process.
- **Abolishing discrimination**: the decision-maker must be impartial throughout the process and must ignore personal convictions and beliefs during the decisional process.
- **Information accuracy**: this rule is based on the ideal that decisions will be made based on precise and concrete information and taking into consideration the opinion of field experts.
- **Correctibility**: a procedural process of straightening out bad calls should be made available.
- **Suggestive character**: the opportunity of expressing one's opinion should be available to the subjects of the procedure.
- **Morality**: procedures have to be based on high ethical standards, without using mischievous or immoral practices.

Furthermore, Leventhal [26] has shown that correctness and equality perceptions in the procedural process are less important than the perception of equity and distributive justice. Lind and Tyler [28] have come to the conclusion that correctness perceptions in the procedural process are noted as being of the same importance if not of greater importance than the results of the processes.[14] Perceptions of lack of equality, transparency, and correctness in the procedural processes, such as promoting opportunities and disciplinary procedures within a company, can have a negative impact on the convictions and legitimacy of organizational processes. Organizations must avoid activities such as discrimination, favoritism and nepotism in these processes. Perceptions of these kind of activities feed the culture of distrust and resentment in work relationships. Fair and adequate procedures within workplace relationships are essential for promoting and encouraging a culture of business integrity.

---

[12]*Ibid.*
[13]Ref. [26].
[14]Ref. [28].

### 4.3.3 Employees' Participation and Involvement

The involvement and participation of employees, known as the employees' opinion, is a constant area of debate in Europe. The employee's opinion can be defined as being the level of participation and involvement the employee has in influencing decision-making regarding tasks and the work environment. It is a subject of debate because it is considered that it reduces the executive offices' prerogatives regarding the best way of deciding the business' interests and its owners. In Europe, the debate is whether employees should have a say in the decisional process and up to which level they should participate in it. The employee's opinion may be divided into direct and indirect mechanisms. Direct, or empowered, mechanisms are those ways through which the employee and the employer communicate, through the authorized individuals. The importance of the employee's opinion, in Europe, can be seen from three perspectives:

- **The moral perspective** (*the moral necessity of the employee's opinion*)—Gorden [18] stated: *Communication is a fundamental social instrument.* The notion of work has its roots in human survival.[15] Employees spend most of their adult lives working in organizations and Gorden's moral point of view was that there is a universal need for self-expression
- **The legal perspective** (*the legal obligation of the employee's opinion*)—there is a legal obligation in Europe for companies to respect employees' rights to be informed and consulted. The EU 2002/14/EU Directive provides the general norms in this respect regarding specific matters related to work and professional life
- **The research perspective** (*the fact that the employee's opinion has beneficial effects on the business*)—research has showed that the employees' involvement and participation in the company can lead to positive results, which include minimizing conflicts, improving communication and high levels of productivity and its retention. Seijts and Crim [39][16] discovered that actively involved employees are more productive than the ones not involved. The former think they can make a difference within the company where they work. The study reveals the fact that management must make involving employees a priority, by identifying levels of involvement and the causes determining low involvement, and it should also invest efforts into eliminating those causes. The expression mechanisms of employees offer management many possibilities in this respect.

A 2004 study[17] showed the fact that while senior executives *acknowledged the fact that it was difficult to quantify the impact of employees' voice, there was a general agreement with the fact that it represented the gateway toward a more open and constructive work relationship climate.*[18] This study states the fact that

---

[15]Ref. [18].
[16]Ref. [39].
[17]Ref. [11].
[18]*Ibid.*

management thought employees' voice contributed to improving performance due to the fact that it generated a better working environment. Spencer [41][19] advanced the hypothesis that the better opportunities of employees to express their observations regarding work tactics were strongly related to a higher employee retention rate.

Participative management techniques confer substance to the concept according to which higher employee participation can generate positive results for the business. Participative management is a process through which the ones affected by the decisions have influence on the decisional process. Stueart and Moran [43] state that participative management leads to the increase of employee motivation and empowerment, which is positively linked to better client service, higher creativity and innovation from the team and greater flexibility.[20] Participative management increases communication, at the same time empowering employees and giving them authority and responsibilities on certain work practices. But participative management cannot be suitable for all workplaces or organizations. Thus, building a culture of integrity within a business requires the commitment of a motivated and involved workforce. Although the employees' sphere of involvement and participation is still undergoing intense debate in Europe, it represents an aspect which must be taken into consideration when speaking about integrity in the business environment.

### 4.3.4 Employee Privacy

An area which has caused intense debate is that of employees' privacy at the workplace. This debate is focused on the ethical and legal nature of monitoring employees' activities by the workplace employers. It is universally acknowledged that employees must renounce a certain level of privacy when they are at the workplace. Moreover, employers must monitor the behavior and actions of the employees in order to ensure compliance with the policies, protecting business' assets and implementing broader integrity within the business. In addition, there can be statutory requirements from the government, demanding monitoring practices and specific industries. Besides all these, the monitoring level is what sparked debates. It is clear that, although monitoring is necessary in order to protect assets and ensure compliance (traits which help promote integrity in the organization), there are issues of an ethical nature in what concerns excessive monitoring. The necessity of monitoring should be stated to the employees. The perception of excessive monitoring will lead to accusations of infringing on privacy and, in consequence, the purpose of building trust and an integrity climate will not be achieved in the work relationship, missing the greater purpose of attaining business integrity.

---

[19]Ref. [41].
[20]Ref. [43].

## 4.3.5 Freedom of Expression and Conscience

Citizens' freedom of expression and conscience is naturally protected in the majority of the states through a legal setting. In an organizational setting, this freedom can come in conflict with the employees' rights of insisting on confidentiality regarding certain operations within the business. These rights to confidentiality are necessary in order to protect the company's assets and ensure compliance in areas such as finances and accounting. Still, there should be policies and procedures to ensure the protection of the freedom of expression and conscience of the employees within the company. The self-regulating purpose of the warning and integrity policies is that of providing internal mechanisms through which deeds perceived as illegal and/or unethical could be signaled. Policies protect integrity supporters, simultaneously providing a mechanism through which a company's integrity is maintained. At the present time, there is legislation reading this aspect in many European states but its application is not highly performing.

## 4.3.6 General Presentation

The discussed themes regard only a small number of aspects connected to work relations. Many areas of such relationships are regulated through the legislation of the European Union and/or through those of its member states and include provisions in areas such as wrongful terminations, the right to an equitable wage (minimum wage), the rights to association, safety and health at the workplace. Employees have rights in this relationship and must insist upon the obligations of the employers in order to ensure compliance of their activity with the law and with the policies and procedures of the company. This relationship has a complex nature and can be riddled with conflicts. Nevertheless, integrity in business is cultivated through it, and is projected outwardly through many of the foreign business relationships.

**Great Place to Work**
**Great Place to Work started when a New York editor asked two business journalists—Robert Levering and Milton Moskowitz—to write a book called *the 100 Best Companies to Work for in America*. This was the debut of a journey which was going to lead to more than 25 years of research, discovery and building great workplaces. The main description of journalists has been the key element in creating a great workplace; it wasn't a prescriptive set of benefits, programs or practices for employees, but building high-quality relationships at the workplace, based on trust, pride and companionship. *Great Place to Work* now operates in 45 countries around the world, having 5500 organizations and representing 10 million employees. Trust has proved to be the main factor which makes the difference in building a great place to work, according to the studies. This applies to all organizations, regardless of national culture,**

activity branch, dimension or age. In 2002, The European Commission asked *Great Place to Work* to initiate a government-sponsored list of the best companies in 15 European states. The list includes sections for the best big workplaces, the best small and medium workplaces and the best multinationals in Europe. Publishing these lists is part of the Commission's strategy of supporting the European economy through successful businesses, desirable workplaces and prosperous communities, which will advance the competitiveness of the European businesses (Source: www.greatplacetowork.net).

## 4.4 Integrity in Recruiting Workforce

*The human resource function of a company has a strategic role.* It bears the responsibility for attracting knowledge, competences and abilities necessary for a business. The function is involved in employee strategic management and development, which, individually or collectively, works to achieve the strategic objectives of the company. Management practices of human resources include promoting, supporting and strengthening policies and organizational procedures, some of them explicitly referring to the expected behavior and stating the ethical standards of the company. One of the main functions of human resource management is that of recruiting and selecting. This involves identifying internal candidates in order to offer promotion opportunities within the company. One of the main criteria of the ethical decisional process is that of correctness. Real or perceived absence of correctness erodes morale within the organization and its integrity. Among the activities that can cause negative consequences in the selection process are: *favoritism and nepotism, discrimination and the absence of adequate processes and fair recruiting/selection procedures.* These activities and the lack of adequate processes and fair procedures project negatively upon the business. They lead to resent regarding the policies and procedures within the company. An elaborate research on the subject of favoritism in organizations has revealed the fact that it tends to be largely spread and to lead to unfair promoting decisions.[21] Fairness, consistency and honesty are the bases on which the ethical decisional process in business is built.

## 4.5 Integrity in the Relationship with the Clients

The relationship with the clients is one of the most important relationships within a business organization. A popular quote in business that expresses its importance is *Rule no. 1: the client is always right. Rule no. 2: if the client is wrong, read rule*

---

[21]Ref. [47].

*no. 1.* This implicitly states the fact that integrity in the relationship between the business and the client is of the utmost importance for ensuring the long-term success of the company. Clients are predominantly external to the organization. This generates a situation where ethical deviations, real or perceived, that appear within the relationship quickly become visible to the general public. The exponential rise of utilizing social networks that has happened in the last years offers extensive opportunities for building relationships, promoting products and interacting with clients in numerous ways. In conjunction with these opportunities, using social networks in business presents inherent risks. The power of the company-client relationships has transferred from the sales and marketing departments to the client. In order to ensure integrity, businesses must be aware of the potential ethical problems that can arise within this relationship. Moreover, policies and procedures to which the personnel must adhere ensure the interaction through the socializing networks that should be implemented.

### 4.5.1 The Importance of Integrity in Business–Client Relationships

The theory of marketing offers businesses the concept of lifelong client value. This concept involves the fact that losing a client due to a perceived lack of integrity will also involve losing all the acquisitions the client would have made with the company in their whole life. Moreover, it is much easier and more cost-efficient that a business retain existing clients rather than attract new clients. In respect to all these concepts, the importance of integrity in the client-business relationship is of colossal importance for the long-term success of the business.

### 4.5.2 Ethical Practices in Marketing Strategy

The marketing strategy is based on the **4 Ps: product, price, placement and promotion.** Smith (1995) comments that *marketing strategies are more and more exposed to public scrutiny and are judged on superior standards,* caveat emptor *no longer being an acceptable basis for justifying marketing practices.*[22] *Caveat emptor* comes from Latin and it is translated as *the buyer must watch himself.* This concept places the burden of responsibility on the buyer's shoulders when purchasing products, as long as the seller does not actively hide the faults and does not falsely advertise, which may be considered a fraud.[23] Consumers' rights in Europe have distanced themselves from the concept. There is now a legislative

---

[22]Ref. [40].
[23]Ref. [7].

setting which targets consumers' protection and offers consumers a better protection. As can be stated from the concept of integrity, compliance with the law will no longer be enough to ensure integrity in business in this respect. The field of ethics usually starts where the law ends. N consequence, marketing strategies perceived as being unethical can harm the image of integrity within a business. Laszniak and Murphy [25] question why marketing organizations should encourage ethical practices and the answer, besides the explicit one stating that this is the right thing to do, it is that *an unethical behavior is able to generate additional personnel, organizational and social costs.*[24] The areas which can cause ethical problems in the business-consumer relationship include integrity problems in the product area, marketing and communication exercises and price policies.

### 4.5.3 Integrity in the Product Area

In his dictionary, Clark and Fujimoto [5] defines integrity as being *wholeness, integrity and solidity*. He states that integrity in the product area can be a source of competitive advantage and that organizations that have constant success in launching products and sales owe this fact to integrity in the product area. This integrity is not only a function of *basic and technical performance functionality*, but also of the cross-functional success of the people within that business. Strong relationships with the suppliers and clients enable the development of products that meet costumers' expectations. They allow business to provide consistency between the performance of a product and the expectations of clients.[25] Minimal ethical standards should guarantee the safety and effectiveness of the product and its adequacy when utilizing it for the purpose it has been created for.

### 4.5.4 Marketing, Communication and Publicity Practices

Ethical problems that arise within marketing, communication and advertising practices revolve around utilizing communication for misleading and cheating. Boatright [3] defines misleading as involving *creating or taking advantage of false beliefs which interfere significantly with consumers' ability to make rational choices*. Manipulative practices are different from misleading, even though they do not exclude one another. Manipulative practices do not usually mislead, but try to persuade by using elements of the client's psychology. Marketing concepts such as *bait and switch* are among the examples. A product is promoted through a price

---

[24]Ref. [25].
[25]Ref. [5].

cut in order to stimulate people to enter the store. This product may not be available or it is usually of low quality. The offer is utilized as a bait to stimulate people to go into the store. Once in, the buyer is sold a similar product, of a higher quality and at a higher price.[26] Such misleading and cheating practices pose even more important ethical concerns when they address vulnerable groups or businesses, and can have the result of questioning the business' integrity, if these practices are made public.

### 4.5.5 Integrity in Pricing

Pricing is one of the areas in this relationship where it is natural to have different interests. The consumer's interests follow the lowest possible price for a service or product, while businesses want to generate the highest possible profits from sales. Although in Europe pricing is an area extensively covered by competition law, there are still situations in which illegal and unethical practices emerge. Four specific areas where pricing policy can lead to illegal and/or unethical practices include[27]:

- **Excessive prices**: defined as *prices set significantly over those of the competition, as a result of the monopoly or market power.*[28]
- **Price fixing**: defined as *an understanding between sellers to rise or fix prices in order to reduce competitiveness between organizations and obtaining higher profits. Price fixing is made by firms in their attempt of behaving collectively as a monopoly.*[29]
- **Dumping price**: defined as *an intentional strategy, usually belonging to a dominant company, in order to eliminate market competition by pricing very low or by selling goods below the minimal production price.* Once this kind of company has successfully eliminated competitors and has prevented the entrance of new companies on the market, it can obtain higher profits.
- **Misleading prices**: the practice of intentionally misleading clients regarding the real price of a product or service. Special price offers will contain hidden costs.

Price fixing is an important marketing instrument for creating and capturing client value. Still, practices such as the ones mentioned above can lead to legal implications for business and can stain the image of a company. Building long-term

---

[26]Ref. [3].

[27]Ref. [7].

[28]Centre for Co-operation with European Economies in Transition, Organization for Economic Co-operation, and Development, *Glossary of Industrial Organisation Economics and Competition Law* (OECD, 1993).

[29]*Ibid.*

relationships with the clients, based on trust, is a key component of business strategies. The lack of integrity within this relationship can have devastating effects on the successful future of the business.

## 4.6 Integrity in the Relationship with the Government and Public Officials

The public and private sector converge on different points, such as public procurement, license applications and discussions regarding economic and social policies. This public-private interface offers opportunities for corrupt and unethical business practices to flourish. Corruption and its perception in this interface result in a higher cost for basic service for the citizens, while also distorting open market structures, preventing investments and undermining democracy, by questioning the state's democratic legitimacy.

### 4.6.1 The Democratic Legitimacy of the State

It can be seen as a function of political equality, government responsibility, and informed consent from the ones governed.[30] Political equality in a system of collective public authority suggests equality before the law and equality in exercising the rights to participate in the democratic workings of the state.[31] The governmental responsibility ideal involves the fact that government must comply with its obligations toward the ones governed and must be accountable to the public. This role of the government in a representative democracy involves mediation between different social groups toward the government is one of accountability, offering proof of transparency during decision-making. The informed consent is based on multiple principles. The first is that a person be given access to information related to that process. The second refers to a person's capacity to understand that information; according to the third one, there must be a situation where the person can decide without being threatened or influenced. Democratic legitimacy is based on these principles of responsibility, participation, equality, and informed consent.[32] If there is a perception within society that one or several of these principles are being eroded by the interests of the wealthy and powerful, it will lead to the decrease of the democratic legitimacy of the institutions of the state.

---

[30]OECD, *Lobbyists, Governments and Public Trust*, Volume 2, OECD.

[31]A. Weale, *Democracy* (Macmillan Publishers Limited, 1999).

[32]OECD, *Lobbyists, Governments and Public Trust*, Volume 2, OECD.

## 4.6.2 The Government's Role

The role of the government can be seen to include protecting public interests, protecting social, political and civil rights, and implementing the rule of law. The government receives a democratic mandate on behalf of the society, being given the responsibility of acting in the best interest of that society. The public expects civil servants to act with fairness and transparency and to manage public resources efficiently and effectively. The public perception according to which state institutions are corrupt involves unequal treatments and can lead to questioning the legitimacy of the institutions of the state. Where corruption acts take place, the government cannot manage to offer the stability necessary in order to encourage investments. In a marketplace economy, the government also holds an important role as an economic actor. Government's interventions are seen as a justification in case of a market failure. The market failure takes place when allocating resources in an economy is not enough, there also existing possible situations where the market participants could be more prosperous without damaging the others' prosperity. This is defined as being *an allocation of resources in such a way that no individual can become more prosperous without another one becoming less prosperous.*[33] Market failures are oftentimes identified with: *externalities, public assets, informational asymmetry and noncompeting markets.* In these situations, the marketplace system fails to reflect the costs and real benefits of these phenomena. Thus, correcting intervention on behalf of the state is considered legitimate. Interactions within the public-private interface appear in the economy through these interventions.

## 4.6.3 The Importance of Integrity in the Business-Government Relationship

As previously discussed, this interface offers many opportunities for unethical and corrupt practices. The lack of transparency in the process that involves public procurement, lobbying and political donations can lead to a situation where the democratic legitimacy of the institutions of the state is questioned, and the perspective on the integrity in business is fissured. OECD[34] admits that the substantial weight lobbying has on the principle of democratic legitimacy. Lobbying different groups from the society can reinforce these principles and stimulate integrity. Still, when it becomes or starts to be perceived as a distorted process in favor of the private interests of third parties, the legitimacy of the state institutions is questioned. Public acquisitions represent an area particularly sensitive to corruption while

---

[33]Ref. [20].

[34]OECD, *Lobbyists, Governments and Public Trust*, Volume 2.

political donations of a company toward the government can generate the perception of direct dishonest influence upon the state's governing policies.

The government can be inefficient when it interferes with the market. This inefficiency is known under the name of governmental failure, where government intervention determines a more inefficient distribution of resources than it would have in its absence. Such a sector could be adopting regulations that lack vision. These regulations can raise business' costs and can lead to complex and inefficient bureaucracy. This generates an environment where facilitation payments and administrative corruption can surpass inefficiencies. While administrative corruption forms such as bribery are prosecuted, legal provisions concerning utilizing facilitation payments differ from state to state. Regardless of all these, utilizing this kind of payments can lead to shrinking the borders of bribery's and facilitation payments' definitions. The ethical implications of facilitation payments must be taken into consideration when high ethical standards in business are aimed for. All activities between the government and the business environment at this interface must be done with the highest transparency and integrity level.

## *4.6.4 Social Capital*

The World Bank defines social capital as being *the institutions, relationships and norms that shape the quantity and quality of the social interactions within a society.*[35] Besides that, the Bank also states that *there is more and more proof according to which social cohesion is critical for the economic prosperity and sustainable development of societies.* Not only does social capital represent the sum of the institutions composing a society, but it is also *the glue which holds them together.*[36] Social capital, to with the human and physical ones, increases organizations' productivity. Within a firm, social capital promotes better coordination between employees and departments. Social capital can also be perceived as useful for partnerships between companies. Trust is essential for ensuring good cooperation between enterprises.[37]

The literature concerning social capital is very vast, the most notable contributions belonging to the French sociologist Pierre Bourdieu. Still, another perspective on the concept, Putnam et al. [37], refers to the way in which this kind of capital can have as a result the strengthening of democracy and the economic development. The author advances the idea that high levels of *civil community* lead to high levels of social capital within a community. One of the main discoveries of a study which spread over three decades, which involved comparing the economic and institutional development of 20 regions of Italy, is that high levels of

---

[35]World Bank.
[36]*Ibid.*
[37]*Ibid.*

trust and cooperation within a community lead to greater economic and institutional development within the community compared to one with lower levels. These communities have overcome *the dilemmas of collective action* (the prisoner's dilemma, the communes' tragedy), due to high levels of trust, reciprocity norms and involvement networks, which led to more performant institutions and economies. It was discovered that those civic communities also get involved in the political life and believe in participation and equality of the democratic institutions.[38] These communities perpetuate a cycle of social capital, which leads to higher institutional integrity levels and economic prosperity. Putnam [36] also states that this type of capital is a key concept not only in building democracy, but also in maintaining it.[39] The business environment and the government are the pillars of society. Corrupt activities at this interface erode the social fiber of the society.

## 4.7 Integrity in Partnerships

In business, partnerships are formed between two or more partners, their skills and complementary resources combining with the purpose of achieving mutually advantageous objectives. Partnerships between companies of different dimensions can be formed, as well as between companies and NGOs, between companies and the government or any such combination. Partnerships or strategic alliances can be classified under different labels, depending on the existing collaboration and cooperation levels.

A strategic alliance can be defined as being *a cooperation agreement between two or more independent organizations, with the purpose of collaborating in order to reach shared objectives. Unlike joint-ventures, organizations which are part of a strategic alliance do not form a new entity in order to achieve their targets, but collaborate by remaining distinct entities at the same time.*[40] A clear distinction between the strategic alliance and a joint-venture is made within this definition. Still, certain classifications list joint-ventures under the broader umbrella of strategic partnerships/alliances. A typology of this kind defines several types of partnership, such as:

- **Joint-venture**: a joint-venture emerges where two or more firms create an independent legal entity with the purpose of sharing resources and competences in order to achieve shared objectives.
- **Alliance of capital**: this takes place when two or more organizations possess different percentages of a company they founded by combining resources and competences.

---

[38]Ref. [37].
[39]Ref. [36].
[40]Ref. [8].

## 4.7 Integrity in Partnerships

- **Global strategic alliance**: a transnational alliance between companies, more and more frequent in the industrial sector. These include alliances between companies, governments, and NGOs.

Strategic alliances can also be classified as horizontal, vertical and cross-sectorial.[41]

- **Horizontal**: these alliances are identified by the collaboration of two or more businesses within the same industry.
- **Vertical**: characterized by the collaboration between two or more businesses from the vertical chain. Kanter [21] has described them as being *value-chain* kinds of partnerships, within which companies from different industries, with *different but complementary competences*, collaborate with the purpose of creating added value for the end consumers.[42]
- **Cross-sectorial**: a strategic alliance within which two or more businesses collaborate, without being part of the same industry or the same vertical chain.

### 4.7.1 The Increasing Importance of Partnerships in the Business Environment

Partnerships between companies have become more of a mutual reality in today's businesses. Globalizing markets and the fast evolution of technology are two of the key factors of the exponential rise of strategic alliances. Alliance partners offer different but complementary resources, such as manufacturing capacities, access to retail markets and distribution channels, financial capacity, equipment, know-how, expertise, and intellectual property. Strategic alliances offer numerous advantages for businesses and have become sources of sustainable competitive advantage.[43] Among the main determinants behind a business' decision of entering a partnership are:

- *The capacity of obtaining competitive advantages by utilizing resources and capacities of partners including technology, finances, human resources and market access.*
- *Strategic alliances offer businesses the ability of expanding faster and of developing more. In a more and more dynamic and unstable business environment, the ability of developing relationships with other companies becomes a key asset of a corporation.* Kanter [21] *names this* collaborative advantage.[44]

---

[41]Ref. [2].
[42]Ref. [21].
[43]Ref. [12].
[44]Ref. [21].

- *Partnerships allow each company to focus on their core abilities, offering at the same time the option of learning and developing their less strong abilities.*
- *Alliances may allow cost reduction through scale savings. Improvements in quality, R&D abilities and reducing the duration of cycles can be reached through alliances.*
- *Rapid access to the marketplace, increased credibility, reducing risks and production chain synergies offer a lot of benefits in a continuously changing business environment.*

### 4.7.2 Integrity as a Fundamental Component for Cultivating Trust Within Partnerships

Although the advantages seem abundant, alliances may be one of the most complex and difficult business relationships. They are full of risks and it is estimated that almost half of them fail.[45] The ability to manage and sustain alliances can be an important competitive advantage. A high level of business integrity and the ability to cultivate relationships based on trust are vital for building mutually advantageous partnerships. Strategic alliances potentially present *opportunistic behaviors* on behalf of the partners. These behaviors include *cheating, avoiding responsibility, distorting information, and falsely attributing partner property*.[46] The presence of integrity ensures trust in an alliance, preventing claims of opportunistic behavior that may complicate an already complex relationship. Perry et al. [35] name five *social links* in what concerns the relationships between the companies.[47] These are:

- **Trust**: it is considered to be critical in the relationships between the companies. As Arrow (1972) states: *Basically any trading transaction contains an element of trust in itself.*
- **Commitment**: the second social link is that of commitment. This relationship is essential for ensuring success in alliances. Kanter [21] states that strong alliances shouldn't adopt a narrow, opportunistic perspective by taking into consideration the financial and the egocentric interest. Alliances should be collaborative and shouldn't neglect the possibilities the alliances offer for the future.[48] Commitment toward creating shared value is vital for building strong alliances.
- **Equity**: trust and commitment are strongly linked to equity, meaning fairness, this being considered a logical *social link* in relationships.

---

[45]Ref. [12].
[46]Ref. [10].
[47]Ref. [35].
[48]Ref. [21].

## 4.7 Integrity in Partnerships

- **Conflict**: conflict will emerge due to the complexity of the alliances. The ability of being receptive and willing to receive constructive criticism, which represents an essential aspect in any collaboration, will allow for negotiation and communication to solve the conflict.
- **Kindness**: the presence of trust and commitment in a relationship and the ability of solving conflicts through fair and equitable means, in time, generate kindness in the mentioned relationship.

One of the main requirements that companies have when deciding to enter partnerships is the ethical positioning of the company they are going to make partners with. The perception that the potential partner lacks integrity in business will lead to the decision that the mentioned company is no longer trustworthy. Thus, the company will not trust its potential partner. Once a partnership is formed, integrity becomes a fundamental component for the success of the relationship. Trust and integrity within the alliances are crucial for ensuring the success of the relationship. Kanter [21] states that the best partnerships aim to fulfill certain criteria, one of which is integrity. Integrity ensures *that the partners behave with one another in honorable ways, which justify and increase mutual trust. They do not abuse the information they obtained and do not undermine each other.*[49]

---

[49] *Ibid.*

# Chapter 5
# The European Normative Framework for Business Ethics

### Sebastian Văduva and Călin D. Lupițu

Society has developed a complex framework of rules which aim to control the activities and behaviors of its members. The ensemble of laws represents the framework which regulates states' governing, governs the relationship between the state and the citizens and the one between individual citizens. When society has rules in force, having the collective consent of letting itself be governed by them, it is said that the society functions under the rule of law.[1]

The law is reflected in the social, technological, political, and economic development of a society. Changes that take place to moral or economic values influence, in general, the legal evolution within a society. Changes at moral or economic values' level influence, in general, the legal evolution within a society. The struggle for European unity has generated a substantial legislative body, which is now the main legislative source of EU28. The previous CE treaty contained objectives with a fundamentally economic character, the objectives related to social politics being secondary to these purposes. Out of the evolution of the community and its laws arose a vast body of social objectives that are now positioned at the center of laws and policies of the EU. Areas such as consumer protection, work legislation, and environment legislation encompass a larger and larger EU society's perspective and offer a legislative setting within which businesses in EU must operate. The legislative EU setting in the business domain advances a general legislative setting for the whole EU28. It aims to regulate behaviors by

---

[1]Ref. [23].

S. Văduva (✉)
Griffiths School of Management, Emanuel University of Oradea, Oradea, Romania
e-mail: sebastianvaduva@emanuel.ro

C.D. Lupițu
Emanuel University of Oradea, Oradea, Romania
e-mail: calin.lupitu@emanuel.ro

syncing laws that offer an essential legislative minimum in Europe. While EU has exclusive competences in some community law rights area, national governments still have shared and exclusive competences in providing laws at a national level. EU member states introduce legislation in areas where it is not provided by the EU institutions and they can offer additional more severe measures at a national level. The UK Bribery Act 2010 is such an example, a national framework law that goes beyond the similar EU legislation. The legislation of the member states can offer guidance for companies within EU28 regarding the current and future expectation trends in the EU ensemble.

## 5.1 The EU Legislation

Better cooperation and political and economic integration was regarded as the method with the help of which the nations of Europe understood that striving to avoid a war in this area can be achieved.[2] The first stage in achieving better economic integration was the European Coal and Steel Community of 1951. This treaty expired in 2002, when its functions have been incorporated in the EC treaty. The EC treaty and the EURATOM treaty have both been signed the same day in Rome, 1957. The main ambition of the treaties was economic integration; still, treaties allowed a more ample purpose that supported the economic integration, meaning *founding a tighter and tighter union between the peoples of Europe by putting together resources to ensure the conservation and consolidation of peace and liberty.*[3] All subsequent treaties have amended these treaties. These treaties constitute, at this moment, the laws and principles the European Union is based upon and are the main resource of the European Union's law.

### 5.1.1 Community Acquis

It is the legal code that applies to the accumulated legislative body which constitutes the European Union legislation. The term *acquis communautaire* translates from the French language as *what has been agreed upon* and *of community*. The treaties the European Union was founded upon represent the main legislation source of the EU. The clauses of the treaties are generally formulated as policies and large principles. The treaties offer EU exclusive competence only in certain areas, such as customs communion or the competition law, while other areas offer shared competence, EU and national, while national governments have

---

[2]Ref. [19].
[3]Ref. [42].

exclusiveness in other domains, such as culture and industry. The EU institutions implement secondary legislation through the authority conferred by the Treaties. Secondary legislation can be implemented through various mechanisms. These are:

- **Regulations**: the Article 288 from the Treaty on the Functioning of the European Union states that *a regulation shall have general application. It shall be binding in its entirety and directly applicable in all Member States*,[4] the preliminary transposition of these not being necessary in the internal law of the member states.
- **Directives**: the same Article 288 of the TFEU defines directives as being *binding, as to the result to be achieved, upon each Member State to which it is addressed, but shall leave to the national authorities the choice of form and methods.*[5] The directives are directly applicable and allow a break for national implementation regarding a common standard, which can be seen as a method of ensuring the syncing of the legislation of the member states regarding the subject of the matter. They allow member states for some the discretionary elements.
- **Decisions**: are specifically addressed to the member states of the individuals and are binding for the ones they address.

The EU institutions also provide recommendations and points of view, these not having the provision of being promulgated as laws. Their purpose is a persuasive one. Recommendations and points of view, although not implemented from a legal perspective, can have a persuasive effect in the decisional processes of the Court of Justice. The tertiary legislative sources of the EU derive from jurisprudence. Many of the decisions of the Court of Justice are derived by interpreting Treaties and secondary legislation. The decisions of the Court have binding character on the member states, including national courts of law. Taking into consideration its verdicts, the Court relies on general principles such as fundamental human rights and equality before the law. The Court does not rely on precedents, but the fact has to be acknowledged that in most of the cases, the Court will not stray much from previous decisions without solid grounds.[6]

## 5.1.2 Competition Law

The internal market is seen as being *the cornerstone of the EU*. Article 26(2) of TFEU states that *the internal market shall comprise an area without internal frontiers in which the free movement of goods, persons, services, and capital is*

---

[4]Treaty on the Functioning of the European Union.
[5]Treaty on the Functioning of the European Union.
[6]Ref. [42].

*ensured,* in compliance with the provisions of the Treaties.[7] This definition leads to what we generally call *The Four Liberties*[8]: *free movement of people, free movement of services, free movement of goods, and free movement of capital.*

The fundamental principle of *The Four Liberties* consists in eliminating all barriers of movement, imposed either though national legislation or private interests. The EU treaties formulate a series of specific rules regarding competition in the EU. While competition law, which acts to narrow business practices, may paradoxically be the concept of the *four liberties*, it aims to ensure a free and fair competitive environment, where strong businesses are restricted from utilizing unfair methods at the expense of smaller companies and consumers. Competition law prohibits illicit agreements and practices which prevent or distort competition, such as power abuse due to dominant market position. It aims to protect the market's structure, making sure that acquisitions and merges do not diminish competition. In addition, it is active in the area of state aids given to businesses. Cartels and other kinds of anti-competitive practices like pricing or merge control are the main issues addressed in this area of law. At the present moment, Europe is paying more attention to refining the existent legislative framework in the area of competition law. As the internal market evolved, competition law was decentralized by the member states. Through Regulation 1/2003,[9] this decentralization took effect and the competition law is now being implemented both at national and European level, through national courts of law and competition authorities. This has led to a higher implementation degree of European competition laws.[10] The evaluation of anti-competition practices of the abuse of dominant positions and of merge criteria is founded on the important criterion of fairness. Fairness and openness are intrinsic characteristics of business integrity. This involves offering support for an open, free market. Compliance with laws which promote loyal competition is centered on the concept of business integrity.

### 5.1.3 Company Law in Europe

With the evolution of the common market and the four freedoms, the European Community has reached the conclusion that the syncing and coordination of the commercial societies' rights within it is necessary. The purpose of this process is that of creating *an approximation of the laws* through which the laws would not be identical, but have similar characteristics. These ambitions were soon to be turned

---

[7]Article 26(2) of the TFEU http://eur-lex.europa.eu/LexUriServ/LexUriServ.do?uri=OJ:C:2008:115:0047:0199:en:pDF.

[8]Ref. [42].

[9]Council Regulation (EC) 1/2003 of 16 December 2002 on the implementation of rules on competition laid down in Articles 81 and 82 of the Treaty.

[10]Ref. [15].

into reality through EU regulations, directives or points of view. Since the beginning of the millennium, the rights of trading societies underwent major changes in the EU. In 2003, the European Commission published a statement[11] through which it aimed to stimulate corporate governance and modernize the rights of trading societies in EU. This modernization was necessary due to reasons such as increased tendencies of the companies to operate transnationally in the internal market, or the expansion of the European Union and the rapid integration of capital markets, or the fast evolution of IT&C. The Commission hoped to use this modernization to increase competitiveness in the EU. The action plan also involved the objective of enhancing corporate governance reports and recommendations regarding boards of directors.

Financial scandals and the loss of society's trust in the integrity of the companies have led to a tightening of the rules in some areas. The previous exploratory approach regarding the syncing of trading societies has been replaced with the in-force provision of creating a modern law standard throughout the entire EU. In 2006, the Commission presented a proposal[12] which aimed to reduce the administrative burden of businesses by 25 % in 2012. This proposal included amendments to those directives, in order to simplify the law. The amendments abolished a series of obligations, in trying to raise business competitiveness in the EU. Strategic revisions took place after the 2006 initiative and on June 18th, 2013 the Commission adopted a statement regarding *the 10 most burdening laws of the European legislation*, identified by SMEs.[13] The Commission has made an objective of revising these laws and solving the main problems regarding them. It has also adopted an action plan in 2012,[14] in order to adapt the European trading societies' rights and the corporate governance's necessities to the issues of contemporary society and its dynamic economic climate.

The 2012 action plan was based on the faith in tighter rules for corporate governance and the necessity of simplifying rules for the European SMEs. The financial global crisis led to requests for greater transparency in corporate governance. The 2012 proposal announces 16 new initiatives, some of which will require a new legislation and other will be communicated through non-binding legislative measures. The key elements include increasing the transparency and diversity of the

---

[11]On May 21 2003, the Commission published *Modernising Company Law and Enhancing Corporate Governance in the EU—A Plan to Move Forward*. This action plan came in response to a previous report by an expert panel specialized in commercial law, chaired by Prof. Jaap Winter, with the title of *Report 31, of the High-Level Group of Company Law Experts on a Modern Regulartory Framework for Company Law in Europe* (Brussels: CEC 2002).

[12]EC Communication. COM(2006)689—*A Strategic Review of Better Regulation in the EU* (November 2006).

[13]Strategic reviews of the regulations and the EC Communication COM(2013)122 regarding the "10 most burdening normative acts in EU law according to SMEs" http://ec.europa.eu/governance/better_regulation/key_docs_en.htm.

[14]COM(2012)740. *European Company Law and Corporate Governance—A Modern Legal Framework for More Engaged Shareholders and Sustainable Companies* http://eur-lex.europa.eu/LexUriServ/LexUriServ.do?uri=CELEX:52012DC0740:EN:NOT.

boards of directors, risk management policies, the necessity of a higher involvement on behalf of the shareholders and investors, and issues like remuneration policies, especially the remuneration of the executives. These elements are based on society's perspective regarding the lack of transparency and integrity in companies both in Europe and globally. Other initiatives include the support given to European businesses by facilitating transnational merges and the growth of transnational opportunities for SMEs. The law of trading companies is a component of the European law, where dramatic changes reflect the necessities and fears of today's society. Simplifying and increasing economic effectiveness are crucial for Commission targets; still, the growing company obligations to transparency and reporting are related to society's perception regarding integrity in the business environment, or the lack of it.

## 5.1.4 Environment Law

Although the EC treaty does not include any specific regulations regarding environment policy, the EU environment policy was established in 1973. Adopting action programs for the environment was the main measure for providing remedies for the already existing environment issues. There were amendments to the treaties, through which explicit environment policies were added. Through the Single European Act, specific environment policies were introduced, such as

- *Preserving and improving the quality of the environment*
- *Contributing to the protection of human health*
- *Ensuring prudent and rational use of natural resources*

Today's society becomes more and more aware of the potential destruction of the environment through illegal and unethical practices. The EU legislation represents a perspective on the many aspects which raise concerns in European society. There are over 200 directives and many normative acts on the environment policy in Europe. Many of the business and industry activities have the potential to negatively impact the environment. Many industries are involved in practices regulated by the environment law on a daily basis. Companies must know the law regarding this area. Integrity involves an aspect through which compliance with the law is necessary; moreover, it involves an aspect through which decisions must be made by taking into consideration the interests of the community. Environment law contains the aspirations of the European society toward sustainable economic and environmental policies. Many of the European laws and regulations can have a significant impact upon the costs and activities of businesses. Regulations regarding pollutant emissions, managing waste and chemical substances can generate high costs in business. When the Tokyo Protocol was signed in 1997, European companies such as BP and Shell joined an international lobby group which put pressure on governments not to sign, ratify, or implement the said protocol code. These companies later quit the lobby group due to pressure exerted by civil-society organizations and because they realized that the EU environment policy asked for the implementation of the protocol within the Union.[15]

Among the first policy and legislation domains the European SMEs find burdening for business are those regarding waste and chemical substances. EU regulations regarding chemical substances (REACH—registration, evaluation, authorization, and restriction of chemicals). A brief review of the main burdening normative acts was carried out. The Commission proposed that even though no modifications in the terms of REACH will be made, efforts should be made in order to reduce its impact on SMEs, evaluated by the Commission as disproportional.[16] The 7th environment action plan has recently been agreed upon in Europe. The program, entitled *Living well, within the limits of our planet,* advances the EU policies toward 2020. The program offers citizens and businesses a necessary long-term perspective on the objectives of the policies which aim to reach the vision of a sustainable European society, with reduced carbon consumption. For companies, the aspiration of being perceived as having integrity and operating in accordance with the environment law sphere is fundamental for daily business activities.

**The Deepwater Horizon Disaster—Gulf Mexico, 2010**
A long list of complaints made against the BP Company as a result of the Deepwater Horizon disaster caused USA's Environment Protection Agency to indefinitely ban this company and its associates from obtaining new leasing contracts on oil fields near USA contributors. British Petroleum was admonished for demonstrating a *lack of integrity in business* regarding the event. The Agency stated that *EPA is taking these measures due to the lack of integrity in business demonstrated by the BP behavior regarding the explosion, oil spill, and the reactions of Deepwater Horizon.* Eleven people died and the oil spill was the largest of this kind in US history. BP stated that it will plead guilty to the accusation of manslaughter, contempt of Congress and other accusations and will pay a record $4.5 billion in damages. The civil lawsuits following the disaster generated a bill of between $5 billion and $20 billion. Tony Hayward, BP CEO at the time of the disaster, was criticized for his reaction and comments regarding the disaster. In one of these, he states: *We are sorry for the massive distress this event caused in their lives. No one wants this thing to be over more than I do. I'd like my life back.* His comment was strongly criticized as being selfish, and president Obama commented that Hayward *would not be working for me anymore after those statements.* In court, Robert Bea, expert on safety management and former BP consultant, stated that the disaster is the result of a *classic management and leadership failure at BP.* The company's culture was subjected to constant attacks during the lawsuit. (Source: *Bloomberg Businessweek.* www.businessweek.com/)

---

[15]The industry founded the Global Climate Coalition (GCC) to lobby against the provisions of the Kyoto Protocol. The named European companies, Shell and BP, withdrew from this coalition. Thus, the American and European perspectives on environmental policies may be seen as divergent on this issue.

[16]http://europa.eu/rapid/press-release_Ip-13-188_en.htm.

## 5.1.5 Consumer Protection Law

Consumers are essential for the long-term success of any business. When they perceive a lack of integrity in a company, they will lose trust in that business or market. The EU consumer protection law aims to increase consumer trust in the market. It regulates what a company can and cannot do. The legislation for consumer protection increases business costs. In spite of all these, as society becomes less tolerant toward unpleasant events incurred from someone else's fault, companies must comply with consumerprotection laws in order to obtain integrity in business. Although consumer protection was not explicitly stated in the initial EC treaty, the Community adopted a program for consumers in 1975, which aimed to implement five areas of fundamental consumer rights. These were[17]:

1. *The right to health and safety's protection*
2. *The right to economic interests' protection*
3. *The right to compensation*
4. *The right to information and education*
5. *The right to representation (the right of being heard)*

The purpose of the consumers' rights law at that stage was to harmonize with the national laws of the member states, with a strong emphasis on avoiding distortions in competitiveness between individual states. Implementing the laws was difficult because they required unanimous approval from the Council, because the Treaties did not specifically express consumer rights. The legislation at that stage included *The Directive on Product Liability*[18] and *The Directive on Misleading Advertising.*[19] Accepting the Single European Act did not specifically introduce regulations for consumer protection. But it recognized the necessity of speeding the synchronization of the laws in order to provide better consumer protection. The introduction of the Treaty on the European Union explicitly contained consumer protection as an EU policy. This required *a high level of consumer protection.*[20] The history of consumer protection laws evolved from their being

---

[17] *Preliminary programme of the European Economic Community for a Consumer Protection and Information Policy* (1975) http://eur-lex.europa.eu/LexUriServ/LexUriServ.do?uri=CELEX:31975Y0425(02):en:HTML.

[18] Council Directive 85/374/EEC of 25 July 1985 on the Approximation of the Laws, Regulations and Administrative Provisions of the Member States concerning Liability for Defective Products (OJ L 210, 7.8.1985, p. 29). This directive enforced the strict accountability of producers for all damage inflicted by defective products.

[19] Council Directive 84/450/EEC of 10 September 1984 relating to the Approximation of the Laws, Regulations and Administrative Provisions of the Member States concerning Misleading Advertising. Directive 2006/114/EC concerning Misleading and Comparative Advertising repeals Directive 84/450/EEC and moves all amendments under one Act. These Acts enforce high business practice standards for commercial entities.

[20] Article 129a of the Treaty on the European Union (TEU), now included in Article 169 of the TFEU.

peripheral in nature to gaining a central position in European law. The increased complexity and competitiveness of the market, combined with the decrease of consumers' tolerance to errors led to a more robust consumer protection policy. Consumers within EU no longer tolerate the *caveat emptor* attitude. In 2012, the European Commission adopted a European consumers' agenda titled Boosting Confidence and Growth.[21] Its strategic vision aims to maximize consumers' participation and increase their trust in the market. The document states that consumer protection policies are essential in achieving the goals of Europe 2020[22] of intelligent, inclusive and sustainable development.

The strategy is built around four main objectives: 1. *Increasing consumer safety*; 2. *Increasing knowledge*; 3. *Improving implementation, increasing compliance, and ensuring compensations*; 4. *Aligning key rights and policies regarding economic and social changes*. Although the laws in this area can generate significant additional costs, the tendency is to have better consumer protection in the EU. The main purpose of this protection is increasing consumer trust in the market. Avoiding the perception of a lack of integrity regarding the future of the market will be central for the companies' success.

**A model of good practice in the legislation of the member states: The UK Public Disclosure Act—PIDA, 1998**

This act offers protection to workers whistleblowing in integrity cases and supports those individuals to obtain compensations for any victimization suffered following their whistleblowing. The act invalidates the confidentiality clauses of work contracts for *protected warnings*. Protected warnings refer to revealing information regarding malpractice. PIDA is an example of protected warning structured on three levels. Once the confidential guidance is requested, a level 1 warning can be made. This protected warning is made within the hierarchy of the organization (protected warning level 1). Depending on the existent proofs that support the warning, PIDA also protects warnings made by regulation agencies (level 2—warning protected by regulatory organisms) and extended agencies (level 3—extended protected warning). The process split on these three level contains a rational escalation of whistleblowing according to its range. Evidence and circumstances must be present in order to justify an escalation of the process. PIDA works by increasing the employees' motivation to improve their risk management culture. This is obtained without insisting on specific requirements in the area. The act motivates employees to protect their own interests, because any external warning can have a devastating effect on the company. Through PIDA, the company has solutions to choose from as long as it takes measures in order to reduce the risk and it does not persecute the whistleblower. The act does not provide statutory punishments through PIDA. In any case, retributions for harassment are considerable and act as a deterrent against harassment.

---

[21] European Commission. COM(2012)225 final. A European Consumer Agenda—Boosting Confidence and Growth: http://ec.europa.eu/consumers/strategy/docs/consumer_agenda_2012_en.pdf.

[22] *"Europe 2020 is the EU's growth strategy for the coming decade"* http://ec.europa.eu/europe2020/index_en.htm.

## 5.1.6 Labor Law

Work relationships are strongly anchored in a thick legislative network at EU level. These laws confer rights and obligations to both sides involved in such a relationship.[23] The EU labor legislation has two major goals—an economic one and a social one. The social one is to protect vulnerable workers. The economic one is that of coordinating labor policy throughout the EU to ensure a minimum legislative level in the member states. This coordination aims to discourage the migrations of companies toward member states where laws, through their nature, can be seen as favorable to the business environment.[24] At a community level, the legislative body provides minimum employer and employee rights and obligations within the EU. It covers **two major areas**[25]: (i) **the work conditions of the workers and** (ii) **informing and consulting employees**. There is also a comprehensive legislation body which aims to provide protection against discrimination on EU territory and affects certain areas in the said employer–employee relationship. The evolution of labor law in the EU has followed a similar trajectory to the one on consumer protection. Initially, the EC's labor law was designed to ensure a fair competitiveness legislation and to assist in creating a single market. As EU social policies extended, labor law began to play an important role in the continuous social improvement aspirations regarding life and working conditions within the EU territory.

The European labor law is linked to the collective vision of member states regarding a society which combines economic growth with the improvement of life standards and working conditions. Europe 2020 continues this vision of supporting work, productivity, and social cohesion across Europe. The EU 2020 program includes such initiatives as increasing the skills, mobility, and access of young people on the labor market. It includes an agenda for new jobs and skills to raise the employability and sustainability of social models[26] *Central to the aims of Europe 2020 are strategies to encourage worker and student training, gender equality, the employment of older workers and the strategy of flexicurity.*[27] The EU legislation provides a substantial body of laws regarding workplace relationships. It is essential that the business environment understands the importance of the laws and obligations comprised in this body of laws and the way in which workplace relationships are central for attaining business integrity.

---

[23]Ref. [7].

[24]Ref. [42].

[25]http://ec.europa.eu/social/main.jsp?catId=157&langId=en.

[26]Summary of Europe 2020: http://europa.eu/legislation_summaries/employment_and_social_policy/eu2020/em0028_en.htm.

[27]Flexicurity is an integrated strategy aiming to satisfy the employer's need for flexible workforce while also satisfying the employee's need for workplace security.

## 5.1.7 Anticorruption Legislation in the EU

EU law contains two specific legal instruments for combating corruption—the EU's 1997 Convention on combating corruption, which involves officials of the European communities or member states and the 2003 Framework Decision on Combating Corruption in the Private Sector.[28] The 1997 Convention tackles the acts of corruption of civil servants, while the FD targets corruption in the private sector. The normative anticorruption framework was developed by EU joining the UNCAC in 2008.[29] The international legal instruments complement simultaneously the EU law, including

- **GRECO (Group of States against Corruption within Europe's Council)**: established in 1999 in order to monitor compliance of the states with the anticorruption measures of the organization. It aims to enable its members to fight against corruption, monitoring them through a process of mutual assessment and social control. It is the most inclusive mechanism for complementing the EU legal instruments, as all EU's member states participate in GRECO
- **The OECD anti-bribery convention**: the OECD convention establishes binding standards for incriminating foreign public officials' bribery in cases of international business transactions. It was the first and only anti-bribery instrument that focused on *the offer part* of the bribery transaction. This convention does not include some of the EU member states.
- **The UN convention against corruption (UNCAC)**: it entered into force in 2008. It is the first global binding anticorruption instrument. It covers areas such as preventing and incriminating corruption and the necessity of international cooperation in fighting against it. The convention also includes the explicit fundamental right to recover assets.

Vast areas of corrupt activities within EU are regulated through these legal instruments. Given the multiple legal instruments, it is surprising that the average EU27 score at that time, according to the Corruption Perception Indicator survey carried out by Transparency International on a 10-year interval between 2000 and 2010, only moderately improved, from 6.12/10 in 2000 to 6.3/10 in 2010.[30] This led to ample discussions in the EU regarding the policy measures which must be carried out in fighting corruption. *The 2003 FD had as its central objective for the member states to incriminate two types of behavior: 1. Promising, offering or giving bribe to a person in the private sector so that he/she will do or restrain from doing something, thus infringing on their work duties; and 2. Demanding or receiving,*

---

[28]Council Framework Decision 2003/568/JHA on Combating Corruption in the Private Sector (OJ L 192, 31.7.2003. p. 54).

[29]EU joining the United Nations Convention against Corruption. Council Decision 2008/801/EC (OJ L 287, 29.10.2008, p. 1).

[30]Cited in the European Commission's Communication to the European Parliament, the Council and the European Economic and Social Committee (EESC), Fighting Corruption in the EU. Brussels, 6.6.2011.

by a person in the private sector, any form of bribery or the promise of bribery in order to do or not do something, thus infringing on their work duties. This instrument aimed to incriminate both active and passive involvement in giving bribery. The first implementation report, from 2007, showed that many member states did not make many efforts to apply it. The second one also criticized the efforts of the member states. Concerning the FDs, the Council does not have the authority to sue the member states, but that changed on December 1, 2014. The European debate also included the possibility of introducing a new directive on the principles stated in the FD.

**The Stockholm Program** led to calls from EU member states for a more coherent and cooperative approach in fighting against corruption in the EU. International instruments, such as GRECO, had limitations in their EU effectiveness, and the Commission introduced the anticorruption report of the EU in order to increase cooperation on the corruption issue. The report will include a call for better cooperation with the enforcement bodies within the EU. The Commission also requested for the public–private dialog regarding corruption in the business environment to be intensified and will support the efforts made regarding these initiatives. Other proposals of the Commission regarding combating corruption include revising the EU's normative setting regarding the seizing and recovery of assets. These laws will make sure that the member states are effectively capable to freeze the assets obtained from criminal activity. A recent proposal of the Commission regarding an amendment brought up with Accounting aims to increase transparency within companies regarding their efforts of combating corruption and bribery. It will target companies with a minimum of 500 employees, which will be obligated to report and publish both their anticorruption policies and their results. They will also have to report on such topics as the social and environmental impact of their business, on other aspects concerning their employees, and on diversity issues. These proposals must be approved by the European Parliament and by the member states to take effect.

## A model of good practice in the legislation of member states—United Kingdom Bribery Act 2010

This Act is renowned for being one of the most, if not *the* most, restrictive anticorruption norm in the world. The key principle companies must endorse from this legislation is that the business environment must have an understanding of the risks companies are taking, then it must document them and take the appropriate measures to reduce those risks. The Act mentions four main crimes, which can be perpetrated in the public or the private sector: offering or promising bribe—giving, requesting or receiving bribe; taking bribe; bribing a foreign official; and the failure of a commercial organization to prevent giving and taking bribe. Introducing this corporate felony stated by the Bribery Act included criminal convictions for up to 10 years in prison, unlimited fines, and the potential ban on contracts with EU member states. The Act has almost universal jurisdiction, allowing the impeachment of British companies which operate abroad and of foreign companies which operate in the United Kingdom, regardless of the place where the deed takes place. The Act does not discriminate between facilitation payments and bribery. The published guidelines regarding the Act specify the fact that there are no exceptions for facilitation payments, any deed of this kind being illegal through the regulations of the Act. This is opposed to the United States Foreign Corrupt Practices Act, which allows *facilitation and speeding of routine governmental actions*. The emerging global tendency against facilitation payments is established through this law, as the application of this Act sets what appears to be the future minimum behavior standard for international business transactions.

**The EU directives on bookkeeping and transparency**
On June 12, 2013, the European Parliament voted in favor of the new Directives on bookkeeping and transparency, which request that all oil, mining, and forestry companies registered in the EU and the ones unregistered in the EU publish all payments of over €100,000 made toward governments, including copyrights, taxes, commissions for obtaining licenses and dividends, no matter where they operate in the world. The Commission has decided to respond to the international developments in this field, especially to the similar laws regarding financial transparency introduced through the Dodd-Frank Act in the USA. The member states must transpose these measures into their legislations by the end of 2015 (Source: http://europa.eu/rapid/press-release_MEMO-13-541_en.htm).

## 5.1.8 Legislation on Public Procurement

Procurement takes place at the borderline of businesses. It represents the biggest corruption vulnerability to bribery, illegal commissions, and inventory theft. The anticorruption legislation covers most of the corruption deeds which appear along procurement processes. The lack of integrity in business dues to corrupt acquisition practices may lead to pecuniary consequences, such as by the loss of reputation. At the EU level, procurement legislation refers exclusively to the area of public acquisitions. Their costs have been estimated at €2.4 trillion in 2010.[31] Governmental activity is considered to be the most vulnerable to corruption. Public acquisitions take place at the interface between the public and the private sector. Transparency, responsibility and integrity are considered to be crucial requirements for promoting integrity in the public procurement process.

The EU public procurement legislation is comprised in the 2004/17/EC Directive[32]—which aims at public acquisitions made by entities which operate in

---

[31] European Commission: http://ec.europa.eu/governance/impact/planned_ia/docs/2011_markt_004_white_paper_e_procurement_en.pdf.

[32] Directive 2004/17/EC of the European Parliament and the Council of 31 March 2004 Coordinating the Procurement Procedures of Entities Operating in the Water, Energy, Transport and Postal Services Sectors.

the utilities sector—and in the 2004/18/EC Directive[33]—which targets acquisitions made by public-service organisms. The Directives impose legal obligations on public organisms regarding the utilized procedures for contracts beyond a certain threshold. The Directives cover approximately one-fifth/€447 billion from public procurement contracts.[34] The purpose of the Directives is to ensure competitive processes made in a transparent, open and objective way, which provides the best price–quality ratio. The purpose of the modernization process is simplifying the older process in order to increase access to public acquisitions, especially for SMEs. It proposes three new directives regarding public procurement.[35] Debates regarding these proposals are centered on the possibility of simplifying procedures and at the same time on the retention and improvement of the elements of the 2004 directives, which promoted integrity among business individuals and public officials involved in the public procurement procedures.[36] The real or perceived business corruption which involves public acquisitions can have a devastating effect on stakeholders' trust in the integrity of the business environment.

### 5.1.9 Legal Instruments Which Target Lobbying

At the moment, there is no legislation within EU which asks for the member states to keep a mandatory lobbying record. Moreover, there is no formal legislation which requests such records at the EU institutional level. There are, however, heated debates regarding introducing this kind of record. Up to the present, the European Commission and the European Parliament have put together *The Transparency Register*, which is voluntary in nature. There is an ongoing process of reviewing in order to determine the optimal way of reaching lobby transparency at USA level. One of the main arguments of the Commission against a mandatory register is that the EU treaties do not contain a practical legal basis to replace the secondary legislation on this matter. The Commission argued that the only potential regulation the Treaties contain is Article 352 of TFEU, which would require a unanimous vote among member states. A recent study claims that another possible method of influencing the secondary legislation would be through Article 298(2) of TFEU,[37] an analysis which the Commission accepted as possible.[38] The law

---

[33]Directive 2004/18/EC of the European Parliament and the Council of 31 March 2004 on the Coordination of Procedures for the Award of Public Works Contracts, Public Supply Contracts and Public Service Contracts.

[34]European Commission: http://ec.europa.eu/governance/impact/planned_ia/docs/2011_markt_004_white_paper_e_procurement_en.pdf.

[35]The proposed Directives are: the "Classical" Public Procurement Directive, the Utilities Directive, and the Directive for e-Procurement.

[36]Ref. [45].

[37]Ref. [24].

[38]Ref. [6].

provides a framework on whose basis trust in the business environment can be built. It establishes a minimum regarding the behaviors the society expects. Compliance with and awareness of the tendencies regarding the changes proposed at legislative level are essential for building integrity in the business environment. Still, integrity is more than compliance with norms and laws. The law can only have a general character, while the specific ethical dilemmas that companies face on a daily basis being unable to be included in it. Laws indeed offer the grounds for the moral expectations of a society; still, the law can evolve slowly even if in a dynamic business environment integrity will obey the letter and the spirit of the law, while also inspiring the moral imagination required to face daily ethical dilemmas.

# Chapter 6
# Developing Practice Codes for Integrity in Business

Victor T. Alistar and Daniel S. Neagoie

Practice codes are voluntary statements which express the values, actions, and fundamental principles of the organization, through which the company assumes the incumbent obligations. These codes have the purpose of offering guidance for the members of the society and can establish specific behaviors requested by members.

*Auto integration*[1] and *the identity of the concept*[2] of integrity state that integrity is encouraged when, through actions, high levels of desires and commitments that confer integrity meet. Practice codes express clearly the aspirations of the company with the purpose of helping employees understand and respect these values and ambitions. Moreover, codes absorb company commitments. The values a company commits to respect form its fundamental beliefs and confer identity. The aspirations and commitments incorporated in a company's practice code can be different from its real behavior. It is extremely important for the integrity of the business environment that the aspirations and commitments of the company be met through actions. Otherwise, the lack of synchronization between them will result in the perception that the business lacks integrity. Codes also have the purpose of empowering employees to act correctly and it inspires them to attain high ethical standards in the decision-making process. They are essential in promoting moral values and commitment in business, thus being the way to establish the

---

[1] Frankfurt, H.G., *Freedom of the Will and the Concept of a Person*.
[2] Williams, B., *A Critique of Utilitarianism*.

V.T. Alistar (✉)
Transparency International Romania, Bucharest, Romania
e-mail: victor.alistar@transparency.org.ro

D.S. Neagoie
Griffiths School of Management, Emanuel University of Oradea, Oradea, Romania
e-mail: daniel.neagoie@emanuel.ro

perception that the business environment has integrity. These codes can be split into various types depending on the information they contain; value statements, corporate principles, and ethical codes/behavior codes[3] are included.

(i) **Value statements**

"Value statement" and "principle statement" are labels used alternatively many times, despite the fact that there are also different traits between them. Value statement can be seen as a support for the company's mission, giving it substance and direction. It comprises the essence of the values and principles of the company. Statements offer an image upon how the ethical aspects of a company are integrated with its principles of functioning. These principles are guided by the moral values of the company. Its value statement can be often identified with the company's mission statement.

(ii) **Corporate principles**

This is a principle which defines the ethical responsibilities of the company and its stakeholders. The principles are, many times, longer than value statements and are emitted in the form of articles. Companies' stakeholders form different categories, including: clients, employees, shareholders, investors, communities, and the environment.

(iii) **Ethical codes/behavior codes**

When people establish practice codes in business, the first to consider are the ethical codes/behavior codes. The ethical codes are much more detailed than the value statements or corporate principles. They vary in length from one-page documents to documents over fifty pages long. The content may include stakeholders' attributions in specific areas, such as conflicts of interests and offering gifts. These kinds of codes provide case studies which offer guidance. In addition, they can also contain descriptions of the disciplinary procedures regarding illegal or unethical actions. These are defined as compliance codes or codes based on integrity.

The purpose of compliance codes is to prevent, detect, and punish violations of the law. They establish strict rules that stipulate minimum behavior thresholds and are based on the intent of controlling illegal behavior and punishing the violations. Criticism regarding these conduct codes is centered on the possibility of promoting a wrong attitude reflected upon those influenced by them.[4] Legal compliance documents can undermine moral autonomy and imagination. On the other hand, the business environment in its dynamics can give birth to complex ethical dilemmas which are not contained in the codes. By replacing moral imagination with the fear of punishment, creative solutions to these dilemmas are mitigated due to the fear of being sanctioned.

Value codes have the tendency of combining legal concerns with principles and values with the purpose of increasing moral imagination. The aspirational values

---

[3]Ref. [34].
[4]Paine, L.S., *Managing for Organizational Integrity*.

try to guide employees to reach high ethical standards. They motivate and support imagination in fighting for high ideals and commitments.[5] Values are fundamental beliefs which offer guidance, shape behaviors, and motivate actions. When a value is labeled, the employees receive information regarding the standards which support those values. In the ethical decision-making process in the business environment, these fundamental beliefs are necessary for the orientation of decisions. A code of values promotes a culture which encourages employees to assimilate integrity and practice it.

Frankel (1989) identified three types of codes[6]:

- **Aspirational code**: defined as a *declaration of the ideals toward which all practitioners aspire*[7]
- **Educational code**: the code which aims *to strengthen the understanding of its regulations with commentaries and extensive interpretation*[8]
- **Regulation code (of normative acts)**: it includes a *set of norms which regulate professional conducts and serve as a basis for adjudicating claims*[9]

Even though Frankel foresees that these types of codes are *conceptually distinct, in reality any unique code of professional ethics can combine the characteristics of these three.*[10]

Ethical/behavior codes can be classified as the following[11]:

- **Organizational or ethical codes**: these codes are emitted at the organization level partly to identify and encourage ethical behavior within the organization
- **Professional ethics codes**: professional groups, such as accountants, marketers and lawyers, must follow the ethical codes of the structures they are part of
- **Ethical codes from the industrial branch**: different industrial branches can have their own code of ethics. Financial-service industries from many states offer ethical orientation for their members
- **Ethical codes of groups or programs**: certain programs, coalitions or other sub-groups can establish ethical codes which embrace the values, beliefs and principles of the said group. Accepting the code is compulsory in order to become a member of the group. Examples of these codes include: The Business Principles of the CAUX Round Table, UN Global Compact, and the FairTrade UK Foundation.

---

[5]Ibid.
[6]Ref. [14].
[7]Ibid.
[8]Ibid.
[9]Ibid.
[10]Ibid.
[11]Ref. [7].

(iv) **Global practice codes for business**

The globalization issue is one of the most debated in today's society. The world has become more and more interconnected, socially, politically, and economically speaking. Globalization was saluted in many circles, especially in the business environment; still, there are sections of the society where the results of globalization were perceived negatively. Issues related to the business practices regarding globalization have been at the center of these criticisms. This precipitated the debate that aimed to determine whether global conduct practices for achieving socially acceptable standards in the business environment are feasible. While national frontiers have been eroded as a result of globalization, the different legal quadrants remained, reflected, for instance, in the various moral and cultural rules observed in different regions of the world. The theory of ethical relativism suggests that morality is a specific and subjective context. In relation with the business environment, it shows that different ethical codes are necessary in different cultural contexts. At the other end of the spectrum, ethical absolutism suggests that there is a universal set of morality; therefore, an ethical code must incorporate all circumstances. The reality is that, even though there are cultural differences, the universal principles and the ethics with the help of which the business environment functions does prevail.[12] The growth, in society's opinion, of immoral business practices has led to important initiatives in searching for the universal ethical codes for the business environment at a global level. These include the *UN Global Compact*[13] and *The Business Principles of the CAUX Round Table*.[14]

(v) **Practice codes for SMEs**

Integrity in business is essential for building relationships based on trust with the suppliers, clients, employees, and the community. The ability of succeeding in auction processes and of creating strategic partnerships with large businesses and the government is based progressively more on social prerogatives and the business environment. The increasing pressure exerted by society, especially after the 2000 corporate scandals and the beginning of the global financial crisis, compels the managements of SMEs to evaluate their position regarding the ethics which guides their business behaviors.[15] The values and principles an SME is built upon are generally self-specific. The actions of the management determine the general character with the help of which the business is guided and the formal codes and programs do not reflect the current situation in many SMEs.

---

[12]Ibid.

[13]UN Global Compact is a strategic political initiative through which the business environment pledges to align its practices to the 10 universally accepted principles focusing on human rights, the working class, the environment and anticorruption: www.unglobalcompact.org.

[14]The Caux Round Table was founded in 1986 by businesspeople of USA, Europe, and Japan. In 1994, their business principles were launched together with the article *An Intelligent Set of Ethical Norms for Business Operating Internationally and in Diverse Cultures*: http://www.cauxroundtable.org1.

[15]Institute for Business Ethics, *Business Ethics for SMEs*, 2010.

Still, the changing business environment offers advantages for SMEs including a formal ethics policy. At the center of this policy will be the building of a code which will create a foundation where integrity business will be built upon. The code will be sent to the stakeholders both internally and externally, in order to demonstrate that the business environment takes ethics and compliance seriously.[16]

Elaborating a code and an ethics program for SMEs will follow the steps taken by big companies in elaborating codes, even if on a smaller scale. Utilizing codes and standards, such as the industrial and external global ones, can complete and improve the policy and culture of SMEs. Certain industries have launched practice codes which deal with specific ethical problems which occur in this industry. Business associations have collaborated with the civil society in order to produce codes which have as purpose improving the ethical standards within specific industries. Codes such as The Business Principles of the CAUX Round Table, which is a contracting business, can offer guidelines for SMEs regarding unfavorable criteria. Contracting business such as the UN Global Compact offer principles which must be transposed in a business code in order to ensure the member quality of the initiatives. Collaboration between organizations of the civil society and the business environment can increase greatly the capacity of SMEs to produce and apply efficient business practice codes.[17]

## 6.1 The Content of such Practice Codes

In order to be efficient, such a code must be elaborated by the company, so it suits its needs and aspirations. The content must be adapted to and reflect relevant information relevant to the environment of that organization. For instance, a company which works in the toy industry must include special provisions in its code regarding children safety. In elaborating the content of the code, it is important that it be developed through consultations with, and the collective involvement of, the employees of all areas of the company.[18] This will allow a better and complete understanding of the daily ethical problems the employees face. It will develop the sense of shared property of the employees over the document. Moreover, resent-based aversions in case the code is perceived as being imposed by the management will be avoided. Business practice codes include, as Frankel stated,[19] the contents of a normative, educational and/or aspirational act.

---

[16]Ibid.
[17]Ibid.
[18]Ref. [34].
[19]Ref. [14].

## 6.1.1 The Content of Value Statements and Corporate Principles

A value statement will establish the fundamental values of a company and will usually provide at least one sentence to consolidate each value. This value statement has an aspirational character. It defines the values a company believes in and the ones that it wants to support. While the value system is thus ensured, practical counseling is not. Corporate principles are normally longer than value statements and have as objective the highlighting of the ethical beliefs of a company toward its stakeholders. The principles contain the philosophy the company adopts in relation to the stakeholders. The content has an aspirational character but it offers a minimum of educational content in providing information regarding the company's stakeholders. The specific content which establishes practical guidance is not included. Still, it tries to motivate, highlighting the responsibilities and commitments of the company toward its stakeholders.[20]

## 6.1.2 The Content of Ethical Codes

They are classified into two: codes based on compliance and codes based on values. A code based on compliance will only have the content of a normative act. Its content will be centered on a set of strict rules which further establish minimal admissible behavior thresholds. These kinds of codes insist on compliance through fear of sanction. The organizations based on fear will not inspire employees to pursue ethical excellence in the decision-making process. In the pursuit of promoting a climate which encourages exemplary behavior, organizations must have an approach which goes beyond compliance. An ethical code/behavior based on values usually includes an aspirational and educational content, as well as a regulatory one. These codes have content which highlights their preoccupation for the law but, in addition, they inspire employees to strive for excellence. Some businesses build separate ethical and conduct codes. The ethical code establishes the values and principles of the organization while the conduct code defines the expected behavior standards. In reality, though, both titles are used alternatively and an ethical/conduct code will contain characteristics of both. Codes have a more detailed character and involve aspects regarding both the ethical position of the company and its practical orientations concerning employee behavior. Also, the code provides the system through which violations of the expected standards are explicitly discussed and the respective disciplinary procedures are mentioned. The content of the codes is influenced by various factors, such as the size and objectives of the company, its geographical position, its industrial branch and its

---

[20]Ref. [34].

## 6.1 The Content of such Practice Codes

cultural considerations. While the content of the codes differs due to the above-mentioned factors, a value-based code will contain the following aspects[21]:

- **The company's mission**: the official statement defines the purpose and the focus of the company
- **The leadership statement**: this statement by the CEO or the board bears the form of a letter. It is important because it defines for the employee the importance of the company's values, and the company's ethics
- **The value statement/relationships with the stakeholders**: this section includes the statement regarding the company's values and fundamental beliefs. If a company has a value statement or a corporate principle, it can be included here.
- **Ethical and conduct guidelines**: in this section are comprised specific areas where ethical dilemmas can emerge, such as conflicts of interests and transactions based on privileged information
- **Specific rules regarding conduct**: while a document based on values will have motivation as its purpose, the code will include, in addition, the prohibition of certain types of staff behavior
- **The list with the means of obtaining advice**: this section offers advice on obtaining counseling regarding the code's provisions
- **The possibility of reporting illegal/unethical behavior**: this resource has a major role in starting a code based on values. It comes with a strict interdiction against retaliation against a person using it.

Codes should use simple, clear, and concise language. Clarity in understanding the content of the code is important. Utilizing active, positive language is essential. Using negative language in the text of the code favors the emergence of resent among the company staff and employees. Company executives and management must get involved in the developing of the code. The values and guiding philosophy of a company will mainly come from the top management. Still, an understanding of the daily ethical dilemmas employees face is vital when the content of the code is conceived. Therefore, top management must supervise the development of the code by consulting, and having collective commitments with, the managers, employees, and stakeholders. This will ensure shared property of the code at all levels of the company. Imposing a code developed solely by the top management of the company may stimulate employee resent.

When a value-based ethical code is developed, positive language which inspires and educates employees is fundamental in promoting integrity and a culture of high ethical standards. While aspirations to values and beliefs are important, it still is essential that the content of a code be realistic regarding what the company can achieve. The commitment to eradicate children labor exploitation across the supply chain of the company evokes intentions most noble. Still, children labor

---

[21]International Federation of Accountants (IFAC), *Defining and Developing an Effective Ethics Statement*, 2007.

exploitation is a complex problem and it can be extremely difficult for small companies to monitor it on the entire supply chain. Therefore, the content of a code is very important in providing information and creating a foundation upon which a culture of integrity will be built. Still, the code is not enough to ensure ethical and legal behavior. The benefits of the code are achieved through communication, implementation, and promotion.

## 6.2 Communicating Practice Codes to the Personnel and Stakeholders

The process of communicating with employees at all company levels is essential in developing a practice code. It has been highlighted that the participation of the company's members to the process of developing the code encourages commitment and creates a feeling of ownership regarding the code at all levels of the society. Although communication in the developing stage is important, it becomes vital once the code is launched. Adopting a code only to keep it on a bookshelf and let dust set on it will not allow promoting the ethical values it contains. Communication and promotion are essential in order to incorporate the provisions it contains.

### 6.2.1 The Management's Role in Communicating the Code

Awareness and constant promoting along, with the general approach of the notion of ethics, are necessary elements in order to ensure the transposition of the management's commitments into the respective code. Communicating the code through the top management is essential for the changes to be made vertically, top–down, and the management must also communicate the standards imposed by the code. Line managers are closest to the daily operations of a company and play an essential role in the employees' socializing, alongside their daily job attributions; therefore, they play a vital role in shaping the understanding of the company's cultural regulations and values, and are very important in giving life to the code.[22]

#### 6.2.1.1 How to Communicate and Promote the Code

New employees must be offered to read the practice code during the orientation sessions. This is the new employee's opportunity to see the document; however, without communication and the proper promoting, it will be soon forgotten. The existing

---

[22]Ref. [27].

employees must benefit from training sessions where the provisions of the code are discussed. Experience shows that ethical instruction is temporary. People forget, and circumstances and responsibilities change.[23] Communication and training sessions allow discussions based on the code and raise awareness on its ethical content. An ethical code can come *to life* through its publishing and also by rewarding positive behavior through the contributions its content refers to. External communication and promotion of the code demonstrate to the stakeholders the ethical position of the company. External editing can be made by announcing it on a website. Moreover, companies can initiate many creative means to promote their code and ethical position. Some companies used laminated cards. Their value statement and mission can be printed on the backside of business cards. Multinationals print codes in several languages. They are placed in a hall of fame, framed, and hung on the walls of the company hallways throughout the entire world. The creative opportunities of publishing business practice codes are infinite and, in addition, communicating them and their active promotion will bring the content to life.[24]

### 6.2.1.2 Six Principles for an Effective Declaration of Ethics

**Write it**: it is fundamental for the guidelines of the business to be written. These transmit to the stakeholders the company's position and signal the importance of ethics in business.
**Build it**: codes must be adapted to the organization's profile or business method; businesses take place in different environments and different ethical matters are associated with these environments.
**Communicate it**: a code must be communicated constantly to both the internal and external stakeholders. The code, no matter how well written, is ineffective without communication.
**Promote it**: without undermining the importance of communication, the code must be actively promoted. Promoting the code using creative methods such as printing it on the back of business cards, in company publications and on furniture actively proclaims the company's ethical position.
**Revise it**: codes must be revised. Its values remain unchanged; however, the dynamic business environment produces new legal and ethical possibilities which will require changes to the provisions of the code.
**Live it**: if the three principles mentioned above—communication, promotion, and revision—are fulfilled, the code will be a living document. SMEs must reward people who follow the code. Rewarding employees who constantly fall short of the provisions of the code with raises and promotions will destroy the ones genuinely following it.

---

[23]Ref. [17].
[24]Ref. [34].

**Apply it/consolidate it**: applying/consolidating the code is an essential ingredient in gaining the respect of the employees within the organization. Respecting people who regularly fall short of the code will lead to an increase of cynicism regarding its provisions. A fair and transparent disciplinary system is vital for incorporating the provisions of the code in the company's culture. (*Source* Patrick E. Murphy, *Eighty Exemplary Ethics Statements*).

In order for these codes to have credibility, violations must be subjected to disciplinary procedures. In the way a positive and satisfactory behavior brings the code alive, discipline violations have a similar but reversed effect. The provisions comprised in the code must be applied at all times both to the management and to the employees. A code adopted but constantly violated by the management will never reach its objectives. The perception of a lack of equality, transparency, and equitability in the procedural process and in the fairness of distributive law will lead to an interrogatory of legitimacy of the code. Adhering to the code at all company's levels is decisive. This denies critique of how the code would only be a public relations exercise and gives life to the values and commitments it contains. The issue of how to better monitor a code depends on its nature. Shorter practice codes such as value statements and principles have aspirational and values characters. They do not include discussions on specific interest areas. Due to the vast nature of the values comprised in these documents, communication and consolidation on each occasion are decisive in obtaining adherence to the code. Ethics/behavior codes are longer and have the tendency of including detailed discussions on ethics areas of interest for the company. These codes offer detailed information on how to manage areas such as conflicts of interests and bribery. Codes of such nature should specify the sanctions and, in addition, should include orientation regarding disciplinary procedures. Applying these sanctions is imperative in order to give authority to the code. Psychology treaties support the theory according to which in a company there is a significant number of individuals who are motivated in having an ethical behavior as a consequence of the existent sanctioning mechanisms.[25] These individuals require authoritarian surveillance, with the help of the code. A company centered on high moral standards does not want for this to be the main motivation the ethical behavior is based upon. However, the presence of transparent, equitable, and active disciplinary procedures is vital for the efficient application of the code.[26] An ethical/conduct code must include a section which supports the process of exposing illegal and unethical practices. The section of the people that warn out of integrity must offer details regarding the process to be followed in reporting these practices. Integrity warning offers a mechanism through which violations of the

---

[25]Kohlberg's stages of cognitive moral development posit a theory on how individuals make decisions. In the pre-conventional stage, an individual decides through self-interest and external rewards and punishments. In the conventional stage an individual will do what is expected of them. The post-conventional stage is reached when an individual develops more autonomous decision-making based on the principles of rights and justice. Very few people reach the post-conventional stage of moral development.

[26]Ref. [17].

code can be monitored. Revealing unethical practices must be encouraged in the business environment, which should respond positively to its members who feel strong enough to follow this path. The processes of communication, promoting, and implementation of the code are fundamental in reaching the objective of creating a live environment which guides and inspires individuals in the ethical decision-making process. The business environment is a dynamic and complex one and the code, due to its organic nature, must be periodically revised. Without feedback and reviewing regarding changes in the legal and ethical business environment, companies will be confronted with the reality of having old and inadequate standards regarding a management which is successful and presents integrity.

# Chapter 7
# Practice Codes for Integrity in Business—Case Studies

Adrian F. Cioară

Citing the following case studies has the purpose of providing examples on how the ethical codes are formulated and what they contain and does not aim to take a stand in what regards the ethical behaviors of the mentioned organizations. The codes are implemented in different contextual situations and their content reflects them. Arranging the code in order to mirror these contexts and the nature of the business environment is essential for success.

## 7.1 Starbuck Standard's Business Conduct[1]

Starbucks started business with only one store, in Seattle, in 1971. Today it operates in more than 60 countries around the globe, with more than 18,000 stores. It is the number one global supplier of coffee-roasting machines and coffee specialties. The ethical code of the company is called *Business conduct standards*. It is a 30-page document which has been distributed to all employees of the company. The content of the code is of educational, aspirational, and regulatory nature. It offers detailed arguments regarding the ethical position of the company and its practical orientations regarding the behavior expected from its employees. It is a document based on values which intend to communicate the beliefs of the company and which offer the required standards in supporting these values. The code is firmly adapted to Starbucks' business line and is strongly tied to it. Coffee

---

[1]Starbucks' Business Conduct Standards: http://www.starbucks.com/.

---

A.F. Cioară (✉)
Griffiths School of Management, Emanuel University of Oradea, Oradea, Romania
e-mail: adrian.cioara@emanuel.ro

shops are social outlets where people go to interact with friends and to escape routine, therefore the business line has a strong human dimension. This dimension is strongly referred to in the code. The company shapes this position in its code through its values and beliefs, which it communicates to employees and stakeholders.

Starbucks' business conduct code starts with a letter on behalf of the CEO—Howard Schultz. The letter is addressed to the employees of the company and appeals to obeying the law and supporting the fundamental values of the company. This states that this code will help the employees by offering them guidance regarding the standards the company expects. It states that *A commitment of integrity, which acts honestly and ethically and in compliance with the letter and spirit of the law, are critical for our continuous success.* The letter sets the tone given by the management of the company and it provides the importance of ethics for the company. The code complies with the procedure of including the mission statement and from here the principles of the company are categorized. The mission is again adapted in order to include a strong human dimension. The principles address the stakeholders of the business and offer direction to the mission statement and the values of the company. The mission statement is full of the aspirations through which Starbucks aims to *feed the human spirit*. It is aspirational in character and it offers an example of the way in which human relationships are the basis of the service Starbucks offers. From here the information is given in possibilities which offer guidance regarding the code. Opportunities for whistle-blowing on illegal and immoral behavior are provided. Starbucks includes a declaration of an anti-retaliation policy, through which it communicates the fact that the organization does not tolerate any victimization or retaliation on an employee which gets involved in divulging the source of information. The code continues to discuss specific ethical situations the employees might face and sets the standards expected from the employees. A code based on values shares its beliefs with the employees and offers the necessary standards in supporting them. These codes must make the connection between the values, standards, and the expected behavior of the employees. The Starbucks code has this approach when it deals with the specific areas mentioned above. It is split into different sections:

1. **The working environment**: this section deals with the workplace environment and the behavior the employees are expected to have in certain situations. The subsections include: how employees treat each other, how they behave with the customers, diversity, health and safety, Starbucks' quality and shoppers' protection, guns and abuse of illegal substances, paycheck and legal working hours procedures.
2. **Business practices**: this section deals with situations the employees might face in their daily routine. The subchapters included here are: compliance with laws and regulations, international businesses, interaction with the government, sales and advertising practices, loyal competitiveness, conflicts of interests, gifts and entertaining, and it also deals with value titles.

7.1 Starbuck Standard's Business Conduct

3. **Intellectual property and patented information**: this section offers guidance in areas such as confidential information, other data or information which are the object of intellectual property, utilizing and keeping the company's recordings, books and financial and accountancy registers, internal control.
4. **Involving the community**: in this section, the company expresses its beliefs regarding environmental issues and those of political and public relationships. The subchapters include declarations of principles regarding their commitment to the environment, private activities, political activities, and public relations.

The above-mentioned subchapters also contain detailed discussions in these areas; moreover, each section comes with examples which aim to educate the employees in each of these areas. Each section's language and structure are clear and concise. The language is active and positive; still, when prohibitions are detailed, the language is vigorous in its nature. The code ends by stating the fact that a violation of the norms comprised in its content or of other applicable standards may trigger disciplinary procedures, including termination of contract.

Starbucks is a large multinational company, therefore the code is long and detailed. The company operates in a complex environment, doing business at an international level, which is why it requires such a detailed code. Still, smaller companies should take into consideration the structure of the document, if they want to base their code on it. The Starbucks code offers a good example on the way a document based on values is written.

## 7.2 The Nike, Inc. Conduct Code[2]

As it has been discussed, codes based on compliance concentrate on strictly following the procedures and regulations which offer a guideline for identifying errors. Codes of this kind can be influenced by high regulation environments, cultural considerations, and also the purpose and context where the code is written. An example of this kind of code is that of Nike, Inc.

Nike is a multinational company involved in conceiving, developing, and commercializing sports items and equipment and their accessories. In 1990, the company was the subject of an ample critical report which revealed precarious working conditions and children exploitation in its manufacturing factories abroad. The coverage degree was extremely harmful for the Nike brand. Nike introduced a conduct code which aimed to attest the expected conduct from their contractual factories abroad. This was the foundation of a larger compliance program which included provisions for auditing the factories they had contracts with.

The Nike conduct code is a short document based on compliance, directed toward its contractual factories that were abroad, offering considerable information to the public in what concerns Nike's attitude. The form and its content were adapted in order to

---

[2]Nike, Inc. Conduct Code: http://nikeinc.com/pages/compliance.

respond to the critics Nike had to face. It starts with a short introduction, which details the working method. The code offers a minimum base which these factories will have to comply with. In the introduction, it is specified that Nike will continue to work with the civil society, private sector, and the government in order to improve work practices. The code links the contractual factories and the minimum standards it contains. The code is split into eleven sections. The sections have bolded titles and are adapted to the working practices from the factories Nike has contracts with. Although the content is not as disapproving as that of the codes based on compliance other factories have, the substance is that of a normative act. The laws of the countries where the manufacturing is done offer the basis for the code's content. The sections include:

- **The service is voluntary**: this section prohibits forced work
- **The employees are 16 or older**: this disposition states the minimum employable age as being 16 or the age when finishing school is compulsory or the minimum legal employing age, whichever of these is older. Employees under 18 are prohibited from working in a risky environment
- **Harassment and abuse are not tolerated**: employees are treated with respect and dignity and are not the subject of abuses or verbal, physical, psychological, or sexual harassments
- **The workplace is healthy and safe**: entrepreneurs must ensure a safe and friendly working environment
- **The impact on the environment is reduced to a minimum**: Nike obliges factories it has contracts with to protect human health and the environment, in compliance with the requirements of the normative act. Reasonable measures are adopted in order to minimize the negative effects and to ensure the continuous improvement in this area.

Other requirements of the code include: the entrepreneur does not discriminate; freedom of association and collective negotiations is respected; paychecks are paid on time; working hours are not excessive; and workforce employment is provided. The code closes with a section which details the obligation of respecting it as a requirement of doing business with Nike. Nike's conduct code offers an example on how the form and content of such a document depend on the context of the business' operation environment. The approach based on values would have turned out extremely difficult to apply in the context of Nike.

## 7.3 The PSEG Standards on Business Integrity[3]

PSEG is a New Jersey, US-based diversified electricity company. It is one of the top ten largest electricity companies. Its conduct code is named *The Integrity Standards*. The seven values expressed by the company are: responsibility,

---

[3]PSEG Integrity Standards: http://www.pseg.com.

## 7.3 The PSEG Standards on Business Integrity

continuous development, client orientation, diversity, ethics and integrity, respect, and safety. These values reflect the expected behavior in business relationships while they are adapted in order to align with daily work activities. The company is involved in the energy and electricity sector, and the values are adapted in order to ensure the importance of the orientation toward the client and employee, and the client and the security community. The tone of the head structures is given by the management's statement of CEO Ralph Izzo. The letter firmly incorporates the company's values, especially responsibility. It brings into discussion the importance the company gives to the obligation of reporting illegal and immoral business practices. Retaliation will not be tolerated. The predominant role which is attributed to it in the management's statement anticipates the importance this value gains in the rest of the document, under the concept of *Speak!* The code continues with a section which states *as a business environment and as individuals, the greatest quality is our integrity*. The process of revealing information of illegal or immoral nature is described in detail. The concept of *Speak!* is introduced and it permeates the whole document with the purpose of encouraging this kind of reporting. The code adopts a similar approach to the one based on values Starbucks has in the way in which it describes information in order to guide employees in the activities and relationships of their daily professional life. Each subchapter is followed by an example which has as purpose educating employees on specific ethical dilemmas they might face. The language and structure of the document are clear and concise and the fundamental values of the company are incorporated across the discussions on ethical and conduct principles provided for the employees.

# Chapter 8
# Corporate Social Responsibility—From Concept to Business Strategy

Sebastian Văduva and Daniel S. Neagoie

In 2001, the European Commission presented the green book regarding *Promoting a European Setting for the Corporate Social Responsibility*, where CSR was defined as being *a concept through which companies voluntarily integrate interests regarding society and the environment in their operations and interaction with stakeholders*. In a strategy updated for CSR and presented by the Commission in 2011, this definition has been updated in order to obtain an easier to understand concept: *the responsibility of the SMEs for the impact of their actions on the society*. Companies are active members of the society, a fact reflected by their relationship with the stakeholders. The traditional vision of a company's objectives is that of maximizing its profits. In this respect, companies generate more employment opportunities, greater consumer satisfaction, while at the same time contributing to the development of social values.

A modern vision of what the corporate identity represents encompasses a large number of objectives which do not take into consideration only obtaining a high profit, for instance:

- *Providing goods and services which consumers want/need*
- *Creating jobs for the consumers, suppliers, distributors and employees*
- *Continuous development of new goods, services and processes*
- *Investing in new technologies but also in training employees*
- *Developing and promoting international standards, i.e., environment practices*
- *Promoting good practices in various fields, such as environment and work security*

---

S. Văduva (✉) · D.S. Neagoie
Griffiths School of Management, Emanuel University of Oradea, Oradea, Romania
e-mail: sebastianvaduva@emanuel.ro

D.S. Neagoie
e-mail: daniel.neagoie@emanuel.ro

© The Author(s) 2016
S. Văduva et al., *Integrity in the Business Panorama*,
SpringerBriefs in Business, DOI 10.1007/978-3-319-33843-9_8

These objectives compel corporations to be responsible for creating values and for a responsible behavior. The notion of corporate responsibility refers to the continuous involvement of the stakeholders in the dialogue and to using methods of evaluating corporate performance (financial, social, and environmental). This approach is a challenge for the management of those companies which try to balance the interests of a large number of stakeholders (i.e., shareholders, consumers, suppliers, employees, local communities, civil society, and NGOs), because they often come into conflict with the shareholders' desire of obtaining big profits on short term. This detailed analysis of the real social value of a corporation is exemplified in the concept of *triple bottom line,* which is part of a modern business strategy.

**CSR as a business strategy**
A report of the EC regarding the relationship between CSR and the competitive advantages of a company in an industry has concluded that *CSR represents more and more a competitive necessity for enterprises, but this component must be integrated in the business strategy in order to become a competitive and effective differentiation factor.* This conclusion highlights the fact that an effective CSR strategy is more and more important for the competitiveness of modern companies. The benefits are increased through the socially responsible actions of the companies and not only by cutting costs, thus leading to developing values.

*Triple bottom line*
It is a concept patented by John Eklington in 1994, with the purpose of creating a new business language which aims to explain developing corporate values as a concept which surpasses the pure economic models of the past and accelerates switching toward the idea of incorporating socially sustainable and environmentally friendly conduct in the values agenda of corporations. The concept has three components: economic, social, and environmental, described by Eklington himself as *The population, the planet, and the profit.*

- **The social component (the population)**: this component refers to the fair and responsible interaction with the workforce, on one hand, and with the society where the company activates, on the other one. The value of the company increases once the society improves its quality, offering opportunities for the formally trained workforce, which then leads to an increased productivity
- **The economic component (the profit)**: here the term *profit* refers to the economic value created by the company, which benefits the society in general. This is the wealth generated by the economic operations when combining all contributions and that is why it is characterized as a net profit for the economy and the community

**CSR in creating values**

- **The increased performance of Human Resources**: increasing employee satisfaction and reducing workforce fluctuation brings long-term benefits for any company. Promoting diversity in the workplace leads to increasing the experience and abilities brought to the company, thus improving innovative capacity and contributing to creating values in general

- **The increased trust of consumers**: there is much evidence to confirm the tight and directly proportional link between demand and the CSR activities of the company, as studies show the CSR indicators to be the element which most affects the image and reputation of a company. It is proven that CSR increases the consumers' level of trust in the industry; at the same time, it represents a key factor in winning and maintaining consumer loyalty and it also creates a valuable trademark
- **Value through innovation**: the multi-stakeholder approach in business management determines utilizing new dynamic and innovative methods for solving problems and it also offers perspective in their approach. By using the determining factors for the society and environment, new working methods, products, services, and processes and new spaces on the market are created, while adding to the value of the company.
- **Trust in the company**: an increased CSR leads to the improvement of the trust level given by the society to the business or the industry, thus creating shared values. The EC sees CSR as an integrated part of the European Strategy for Development and Workforce Employment, contributing to the increase of competitiveness across the European Union.

**The role of the government in CSR**

CSR is mainly a voluntary management activity conducted in the own interest of the corporations, but under these circumstances a question arises: why does promoting CSR activities represent an interest for the decision-makers in the government? Reinhard Steurer, from the University of Wien, has determined a series of reasons for which the governments are interested in, and get actively involved in, promoting CSR activities:

- The CSR efforts can help **achieve the governmental policies' objectives** voluntarily. This motivation does not have to do only with sustainable development and environment protection, but also with achieving some objectives related to external policies, such as human development, humanitarian assistance, and development assistance;
- CSR policies can be seen as a **set of explanations for the regulations imposed by the imperative norms** in cases where new regulations are not wanted or feasible from a political point of view. In comparison with the regulations imposed by the imperative norms, the flexible character of the CSR policies suggest a comparatively lower political cost in what concerns the resistance imposed by different groups of interests;
- The flexible approach of CSR policies represents distancing oneself from the hierarchical regulation toward another one, based on creating partnerships and self-regulation networks and/or co-regulation ones. This concept of new governance is tightly linked to the concept of CSR, because it highlights the social role private industries play in the public life.

## 8.1 The Government as a Facilitator

In the CSR policies of the European Commission, it is stipulated that no replacement of the legislation external to the industry the company is part of, or of the environment regulations, should appear. It is desired that CSR represents a way through which enterprises overcome, voluntarily, the limits imposed by these regulations in an innovative and productive way. Thus, it must be mentioned that the role of the legislation in terms of CSR must only be that of a facilitator. This facilitation is done through the provisions of the directives and guidelines for CSR through which enterprises can develop strategies and can measure progress based on the standards offered by the regulating authorities. The CSR directives and principles, internationally acknowledged, are specified in the OECD guidelines for multinational enterprises, in the ten United Nations Global Compact principles and within the ISO 26000 standard regarding the Guidelines for Social Responsibility. Moreover, the European Union's policy is to build on this framework at a global level the best practices in a European context. The mechanisms used by the governments in promoting CSR are analyzed in detail in the following sections.

### *8.1.1 The European Standards and Guidelines*

One of the main methods for promoting practices for sustainable business is that which uses as reference the provisions of the standards and guidelines internationally accepted for the companies. Many of these standards are supported by regulation institutions such as United Nations Global Compact or the ISO Standard for Social Responsibility. Within this study, the CSR elements supported by the European Commission will be analyzed as they have been set in the green book published in 2001. These guidelines have been set in accordance with the OECD guidelines for multinational enterprises, the United Nations Global Compact, and the ISO 26000 standard for Social Responsibility. Since 2001, these CSR elements have represented important subjects pointed out in the debates for the development of European Policies.

**The internal dimension**

- **Human resources (HR) management**—a valid CSR policy should include provisions for chance equality in the recruiting procedures, paycheck equality, and strategies that aim to facilitate the continuous development of the employees
- **Work security and safety**—maintaining a safe and healthy working environment for the employees is vital for the CSR concept. A CSR policy should offer a detailed plan which ensures a healthy and stress-free working environment for the employees
- **Adapting to changes**—long-term sustainability of a business is the key aspect in CSR. A code for good CSR practices should highlight the commitment for sustainable business practices in order to offer peace to the stakeholders, who rely on the continuity of organization's activity

- **The management of the impact on the environment and resources**—care toward environment must occupy a central place in the CSR strategy of every company. Ethics codes must include the commitment of the company to reduce the impact it has on the environment

**The external dimension**

- **Local communities**—being aware of the place the company occupies in the community is an extremely important part of the CSR policies. Many companies see a benefit in taking action in order to ensure the wellbeing of the community they work in. Usually they act by sponsoring different community groups, local sports teams, etc.
- **Business partners, suppliers and consumers**—the commitment for building a lasting relationship with business partners and suppliers reduces the complexity and the costs, while offering, at the same time, trustworthy services toward consumers. Guaranteeing ethics in the management of the supply chain is a central dimension in CSR
- **Human rights**—communicating the strategies which ensure that human rights are respected by the company, as the result of its activity is crucial in any CSR policy. Developing methods of preventing corruption within the company is also extremely important for the CSR policies
- **Global environment issues**—increasing the use of harmful fuels leads to the increase of temperature across the globe, thus leading to unpredictable meteorological phenomena, creating an important risk for the most vulnerable inhabitants of the planet, and the commitment taken by a company regarding reducing its negative impact on these climatic changes should constitute a central part of the CSR actions.

## *8.1.2 Promoting CSR in the European Member States[1]*

Steurer (2010) offers an analysis framework in order to argue the ways in which public policies can be used in order to promote CSR actions. This setting is split into four main themes, which cover fundamental areas in which the central authorities can have an influence on the activities of a company, as follows:

- *Raising the awareness and building the capacity of the companies which run their activity in that particular state*
- *Improving transparency and access to public information in all business sectors*
- *Encouraging socially responsible investments*
- *Respecting ethical standards in the process of public procurement*

(i) **Raising the awareness and building the capacity of the companies for CSR activities**—it was proven that there are various methods used within companies which aim to increase awareness in order to impact the environment. Some of the most important are: financing research and educational

---

[1]*Unless otherwise stated, the following sections are based on Steurer's (2010) research.*

activities regarding CSR; creating databases in order to keep the information and report resources in a format open to the public, such as the webpage of CSR Europe. There are also guidelines supported by the central authority in order to offer a national perspective built from international standards adapted to local requirements, such as the German Corporate Governance Code (GCGC) and national campaigns as the Danish CSR campaign *Our common concern*. Sometimes both economic and legal motivations are involved in this process. In what concerns legal motivations, some examples come from the French reform of the law, where a book called *Charter for the Environment* was attached to the Constitution, allowing a constitutional basis for sustainable development to exist in France, which led to giving an increased attention to CSR in the commercial law.

(ii) **Improving transparency and access to public information**—reporting and labeling CSR and also involving stakeholders are the main improvement methods in what concerns the access to information held by corporations and in raising awareness. These methods are used by governments in order to complement legislations; for instance, in France there are the so-called *nouvelles régulations économiques* (NRE)—the new economic regulations—which oblige French publicly traded companies to include information concerning social and environmental aspects in their annual reports. There are similar laws in Denmark, the Netherlands, Sweden, and Spain. Other instruments include publishing the national CSR guidelines and facilitating organizing forums for the stakeholders. Certified CSR labels for the companies are often one of the most important instruments for encouraging transparence in corporations. Labels combine informational characteristics (for the consumers) with economic motivations for the companies (marketing). There is a multitude of CSR labels, both national and international, such as *Blue Angel* of Germany, *Eco-label* of Europe, *Fair Trade* of the UK, and others.

(iii) **Socially Responsible Investments (IRS)**—IRS is an important mechanism for CSR activities, because it incorporates aspects that have to do with responsible business practices as central elements of shareholder capitalism (Moon, 2007). The legal initiatives which support IRS have been implemented in some EU member states, especially in Belgium, where investors are prohibited from making any kind of investment in an organization which has to do with cluster munition mines or anti-personnel mines. The IRS laws also exist in Sweden, where the National Pension Fund is required to present an annual business plan through which it demonstrates how environmental and ethical issues are approached in the investments they make and how these investments impact the management of the Pension Fund. A similar example is the one of the French Pension Reserve (*Fonds de réserve pour les retraités, FRR*). **The Dutch Strategy of Social Responsible Funds**[2] is an

---

[2]The Dutch Green Funds Scheme.

instrument which facilitates *green*[3] investments (*socially responsible*) in certified projects which meet the environment standards (such as *green technology*[4]) through tax exemption for creditors and debtors. The informational instruments which promote IRS include the webpage of the Austrian government www.gruenesgeld.at (*Green Money*) and the Dutch *Sustainable Money Guide*.

(iv) **Public procurement**—governments can develop a multitude of actions in order to increase sustainable development and CSR actions in order to integrate them in the activities of public enterprises. This is done best in promoting sustainable public procurement. There are two EU directives on this matter which offer the possibility of taking into consideration legal or social criteria within the specifications they have. One of these directives *clarifies the method through which contracting authorities can contribute to the protection of the environment and promoting sustainable development, while ensuring the possibility of obtaining the best cost-benefit indicator for these contracts* (L134/114). A survey conducted at European level has demonstrated that the majority of the EU member states have renewed their legislation regarding public acquisitions in agreement with the directives.

(v) **CSR promoting patterns**—the states chosen for this research are Sweden, Great Britain and France, mostly due to their positions as worldwide leaders in what concerns CSR policies but also for the diversity of social assistance models: the Scandinavian, the Anglo-Saxon and the Mediterranean social aid. We feel that through this example we will offer a clear and compact image on how CSR is applied in various governance forms. The data collected for these studies mainly comes from a study done by a group of high-rank representatives of the member states for CSR. Each case study is presented using a summarized system of the key aspects from the elaboration process of CSR policies, described below: *The Understanding of CSR within each state; national CSR strategies overall; CSR visibility for the public, within NGOs and within business communities; methods of reporting which facilitate comparisons between states in what concerns CSR activities; socially responsible investments in the financial sector and in the practice of public procurement; promoting CSR for companies operating outside the borders of the state.*

---

[3]Green investments.
[4]Green technology.

| State | National strategy | Visibility | Transparency and report | Financial sector and public procurement | The activities of companies outside state's border |
|---|---|---|---|---|---|
| Sweden (Ministry of Foreign Affairs) | Environment legislation is concentrated on CSR | The *Globalt Ansvar* partnership between the government and the business environment supports CSR research, consulting, and networking | Private companies must report regarding the consequences their operations have on the environment | Public pension funds must meet the ethical and environmental standards. National prizes promote green public acquisitions (socially responsible) | *Globalt Ansvar*, the Swedish global responsibility partnership, asks members to adhere to the OECD standards and UN Global Compact principles |
| Great Britain (Ministry of Trade and Industry) | CSR represents an integrated part of the business competition policy | The government hosts on its website a page dedicated to CSR. The Queen distinguishes companies depending on their efforts in different interest areas, including sustainability | The Social Responsibility Law (2004) requires companies to publish annual sustainability reports | Pension funds are required to list the CSR aspects of their investment strategies. Public acquisition agencies are one of the most socially responsible within Europe | The Ethical Trading Initiative contributes to improving working standards in the textile industry. Created to add transparency to the natural resources exploitation industry |
| France (Ministry of Labor) | The national strategy for social responsibility supports CSR activities | The Friends of Global Pact Forum: largest international alliance of members enlisted in the UN Global Compact movement | Companies with a great impact on the environment need to report regarding their impact on the environment | Grenelle's law offers the possibility of saving plans for corporations which offer their employees the possibility of owning a part of the company. The national public acquisition action plan offers guidelines to public buyers | Sustainable development is fully integrated in the overseas development agenda, including social and environmental issues of portfolios |

## 8.2 Case Study: Sweden

Country profile: Sweden
Full name: The Kingdom of Sweden
Capital: Stockholm
Population: 9.4 million
Surface: 449,964 mi$^2$
Official language: Swedish
Official religion: Christianity
Life expectancy: 80 years (men), 84 years (women)
Monetary unit: 1 Swedish crown (krone)
Main exported products: machines, paper products, chemicals
GDP per capita: US $50,110

### 8.2.1 The Understanding of CSR

The Swedish CSR approach is strongly influenced by responsible trading and environmental criteria. Social aspects have gradually become part of the national CSR strategy, being traditionally associated with tripartite partnerships between the government, unions, and employers. Sweden started to promote the CSR idea and implement it in numerous state enterprises much earlier than other European states. A dialogue was initiated in 1979 between the industry, unions, and other actors involved in workforce recruiting and its purpose was in compliance with the OECD on its Multinational Enterprises guidelines. The Swedish strategy is based on the idea of motivation and supports voluntary participation of stakeholders. On the other hand, the government launched several initiatives in order to involve the stakeholders. Awareness campaigns of the CSR effects are spread in Sweden. NGOs diligently monitor if companies comply with the agreements.

### 8.2.2 National Strategies

In 1999, the Swedish government took an important step toward setting a coherent framework in the environment area. Fifteen laws regarding the environment have been consolidated within the Environment Code. This reform made a more comprehensive and strict legal environment code, oriented toward sustainable development. The aim of the code is to consolidate performance and objective management. In the past, companies weren't required to reduce greatly the environment pollution degree, while now the law defines exactly the minimum environment pollution reduction standards for the companies. As it is an export-oriented state, Sweden's CSR public policy is generally focused on projecting

CSR concepts in the exterior, especially promoting the agenda regarding human rights of the national government. By far the most extended public policy initiative for promoting CSR comes from the Swedish *Globalt Ansvar* group, or the Swedish Global Responsibility Partnership. This partnership is comprised of four Swedish government ministries, which act as a national nucleus for the CSR activity and for promoting public policies in the world. The purpose of this partnership is to transform Swedish companies which operate outside the borders into ambassadors for the CSR Swedish policy. The agenda of this public policy can be split into four pillars: anticorruption, human rights, working standards, and environmental standards. This acts as a hybrid instrument for raising awareness and CSR capacity and which reaches its target under the international guidelines of the OECD framework for Multinational Enterprises. Many of these activities are actually run by Swedish embassies and consulates, making this state an important player in proliferating good CSR practices in the world. The activity of *Globalt Ansvar* has been discussed by a large number of third-party rating agencies, offering Sweden the opportunity of being ranked number one in the 2007 *Index for Responsible Competition*, a document created by the sustainable development monitoring NGO *AccountAbility*.

## 8.2.3 Visibility

The *Globalt Ansvar* initiative supports CSR research, consulting, and networking and continuous education for managers, union members, politicians, and NGOs members. Twelve companies adhered to this partnership starting December 2003. As *Globalt Ansvar* members, companies are required to produce annual reports concerning compliance with the OECD's Multinational Enterprises guidelines and the UN Global Compact principles. Sweden is also a top country, along with France, in what concerns implementing the UN Global Compact principles. Sweden stands out, along with Holland, as to the degree of compliance with the OECD standards. The Swedish Consumer Agency does activities which have as ultimate goal raising awareness regarding CSR actions. This carries out activities of public relations concerning CSR by organizing round tables and by carrying out studies concerning sustainable consumption, actions which have a global perspective.

## 8.2.4 Transparency and Reporting

Since 1999, large publicly traded companies have been required to report their impact on the environment due to their economic activity in their financial reports—more than 20,000 companies obey this rule. Concerning strictness with environmental issues, there is a sole obligation in Europe. Companies which do not meet the CSR requirements must pay a €500 fine and risk prosecution. Since January 2008, Swedish state companies were required to publish a sustainability report in compliance with the guidelines of the Global Reporting Initiative (GRI). These sustainability reports must be evaluated from the quality point of view by independent auditors. Reporting in the case of state companies does not take into account their size or the industry they are a part of and it is based on the principle of *comply or explain*. The financial report must mention how the GRI directives are implemented and to explain any differences which may appear. Environmental, social aspects, and corporate governance reports of the state companies have significantly increased to more than 94 % of companies publishing these GRI reports. Sweden is now the second country of all European member states in what concerns the published GRI reports.

## 8.2.5 The Financial Sector

The IRS is a highly developed concept in Sweden. Starting with 2000, public pension funds were allowed to invest in companies which meet certain ethical and environmental standards. The Finance ministry monitors the companies' compliance with the law. Thus, the Swedish public policy regarding IRS is seen as a public policy for the management of the public pension funds. In 2000, five political parties approved the Public Pensions Funds Act. This requires all National Pension Funds to make an annual business plan through which they raise awareness regarding the ethical and environmental issues that are taken into consideration in the pension fund investment activities, as well as the impact these have on the management of the funds. In 2007, four of the six funds created the Common Ethics Council, which carries out the dialogue on CSR issues with the companies whose pension funds they are interested to invest in. The Council publishes recommendations for the companies and the pension funds, and if it reaches the conclusion that a company does not obey the CSR principles of the Council, the pension funds can decide to sell the titles owned in that company.

## 8.2.6 The Public Procurement Process

In what concerns Responsible Public Procurement, national prizes proved to be an efficient method through which Sweden encouraged RPP. The reason behind these prizes is that of launching a feeling of competition between contracting agencies and making a good reputation for RPP practices. Since 2008, the Swedish Environmental Management Council offered two prizes annually for buyers and suppliers: *Excellent green purchaser* and *Excellent green supplier*. The awarding ceremony is organized at an annual conference on RPP that takes place in Stockholm. The purpose of this ceremony is that of highlighting positive examples on both sides, both from the buyer's point of view and the supplier's, which work hard and innovatively with the idea of RPP. Moreover, along with the statue, winners receive the right of using the symbol of the prize in their marketing campaigns.

### 8.2.7 CSR and SMEs

SMEs make up for 99.7 % of the total existing companies on the Swedish market, which is very close to the EU average of 99.8 %. For the last two decades, the attention given to the industrial public policy shifted from large enterprises and individual sectors to small enterprises and entrepreneurship. The main reason for this phenomenon is that the SMEs have become increasingly more important in what concerns their contribution on the labor market and economic growth of the state due to the effects of globalization and the rationalization of the operations large companies face. One of the main methods used by the Swedish government in order to promote CSR on SME level takes the form of a partnership between neighboring states in the Baltic region, which takes the name of SPIN (*Sustainable Production through Innovation and Small and Medium Sized Enterprises in the Baltic Sea Region*). The purpose of the project is to share experiences in order to promote innovative solutions for sustainable development, including eco-innovation, environment technologies, and CSR. In the context of innovation, CSR is close to the supply and demand perspective, due to the fact that many SMEs do not have access to new environment technologies, whereas other SMEs which develop those innovative environment technologies and innovative management solutions cannot find profitable markets. The activities of the partners concentrate on:

- *Identifying and satisfying SMEs' needs through a method which avoids noncompliance with supply and demand regarding sustainable development innovations*
- *Developing and testing innovation rationalization and implementation system for sustainable development within SMEs*
- *Identifying and testing adequate motivations for SMEs in order for these to implement the innovation for sustainable development*
- *Ensuring cohesion in creating an international setting in the interest area of promoting innovation for sustainable development between SMEs of the Baltic region countries*

### 8.2.8 The Activities of Companies Outside State Borders

Companies which apply for loans for the public sector are informed regarding the OECD guidelines on Multinational Enterprises. In compliance with the Swedish tradition, tripartite partnerships have representatives from all sectors—government, employees, and unions—working together. Nevertheless, Sweden, as many other European countries, is reluctant to tie export credits, guarantees for loans and investments with environmental, social, and human rights standards. Still, the Swedish CSR vision goes more profoundly than fair trade and socially responsible supply chain. For instance, Swedish companies are encouraged to contribute to the infrastructure of developing countries through public–private partnerships in areas such as local development or energy providing. The Swedish Development International Agency (SDIA) also encourages Swedish industrial associations to cooperate with developing countries. SDIA also supports the quality of agriculture labels.

## 8.3 Case Study: Great Britain

Country profile: Great Britain
Full name: The United Kingdom of Great Britain and Northern Ireland
Capital: London
Population: 62.4 million
Surface: 242,514 km$^2$
Official language: English
Official religion: Christianity
Life expectancy: 78 years (men), 82 years (women)
Official currency: Pound Sterling (GBP)
Main exported products: manufactured goods, chemical industry products, food
GDP per capita: US $38,370

### *8.3.1 The Understanding of CSR*

In comparison to other EU member states, Great Britain has recorded the biggest progress in CSR. At the end of the 1990s, PM Tony Blair showed interest in CSR and created a new model of integrating businesses in elaborating public policies in the United Kingdom. The first work group was named *the New Deal Task Force* and was comprised exclusively of business environment and NGOs representatives. This strategy achieved, from its foundation until present, new methods of modeling and implementing public policies and led to an important increase of the involvement of organizations of the private sector in areas such as education, health, social homes, and pensions. Another important characteristic of Great Britain is the high level of professionalism demonstrated by NGOs, for instance *Amnesty International* and *World Wildlife Fund*, organizations which mainly do monitoring activities.

## 8.3.2 National Strategies

British government's policy regarding CSR is very visible and strong. One reason why this is happening is their strong tradition of unions, and another important one is the pressure exerted on government by numerous campaigns by the civil society. At the same time, the British government sees CSR as a voluntary commitment on behalf of enterprises and encourages them to take it by using the legal argument concerning the economic self-interest, or *the case for business* for CSR. Besides promoting social, economic and environmental benefic activities, UK government's strategy has as purpose cooperating with the business environment, local councils, unions, consumers and other stakeholder groups. Special attention is given to promoting an innovative approach and to the definition of appropriate minimum performance.

## 8.3.3 A CSR Source: Great Britain's Department of Trade and Industry

Between 2002 and 2008, this department created a special CSR ministry, establishing the CSR component as the main element of any general business strategy. One of the main tasks of the minister is that of creating a standardized framework for reports and social and environmental certifications. In October 2004, Nigel Griffiths was appointed the fourth CSR minister, announcing in 2005 the publishing of an International Strategic Framework, which defined the purposes and priorities of UK's government as well as the efforts made by it in granting greater importance to CSR at international level. The strategy focuses on increasing British companies' contribution to the economic, social, and environmental development. The Department initiated the SIGMA Project (*Sustainability Integrated Guidelines for Management*), a project completed in 1999 in partnership with the British Institute for Standards and The Forum for the Future and Accountability. Their collaboration yielded the SIGMA Directives for Sustainable Management, which were then updated in 2003.

## 8.3.4 The Activities of the Other Ministers

*The Department for International Development* also runs an extended CSR policy. It provides approximately 40 % of the funds for the Ethical Trading Initiative. It also applies CSR concepts mainly in fighting against poverty. The Department for Environment, Food and Rural Affairs is more active in what concerns developing directives for environment reporting and promoting sustainable consumption and production. The Foreign and Commonwealth Office, along with the British

Foreign Affairs Minister, also supports CSR activities, which are perceived as corporate citizenship. The Global Citizenship Unit, responsible for matters concerning CSR, has developed, among others, with the help of these institutions, the Voluntary Principles on Security and Human Rights in the Extractive Industry and organizes periodical conferences on corporate citizenship. FCO also supports the Business Leaders Initiative on Human Rights, an association created with the joining of large British companies which managed to integrate the protection of human rights in their management strategies. Founded in 2003 for an initial period of three years, the initiative cooperates at the moment with UN Global Compact and the UN's Human Rights Commission to develop directives regarding the implementation of human rights in the management strategies of companies. The department for workforce and pensions promotes CSR objectives by supporting the Investors in People Standard, which was developed by British companies and unions in 1990. The national standard is an adequate instrument for improving corporate performance through training and personal development sessions.

## 8.3.5 Compulsory Report

In 2004, the British Parliament passed regulations concerning corporate responsibility. The most important consequences of this new legislation were that British organizations were legally required to publish an annual sustainability report. Moreover, the law enhances the responsibility of companies' executives for the society the company operates in and also for the environment. Also, British companies or their offices become liable to paying damages for abuses against human rights or against the environment perpetrated outside the Kingdom's borders.

## 8.3.6 Visibility

Communicating CSR is done through a professional and extremely visible manner in the UK. The government keeps a webpage dedicated exclusively to this purpose: www.csr.gov.uk. This contains a large number of links to other pages dedicated to CSR. In 2004, Stephen Timms, the CSR minister at that time, founded the CSR Academy. Among the responsibilities there is the obligation of proving the business case for CSR. It also offers seminars on CSR themes for the members of the executive boards of companies. The prizes and their ranking represent an extremely important contribution to raising CSR awareness in the UK among the members of society. An extremely important and prestigious distinction for the companies is represented by the Queen's Awards for Enterprise, granted on three levels: International trade, Innovation, and Sustainable Development. This distinction can be awarded for a sustainable product or service or for a sustainable management of resources and relations. Also, the prize does not have to do with the general performance of the company. Among with the BITC (Business in the Community), the Trade Department developed the Index of Corporate Responsibility, which offers companies the opportunity to compare their recorded performances in CSR against those of their competitors. Moreover, the Trade Department and BITC publish quarterly a summary of their latest research in CSR.

## 8.3.7 Transparency and Reporting

Compared with the other European states, UK continues to publish an impressive number of sustainability reports. This comes as a consequence of the debates regarding the Social Responsibility Law in 2004, following which all British companies were legally required to annually publish sustainability reports. The companies received support from DEFRA in elaborating a system for environment management and developing environment reports. In January 2006, following a consulting period of three months, DEFRA published new directives regarding reporting on environmental issues. These new directives were developed with the purpose of helping companies identify the most important performance indicators which could offer the opportunity of managing and efficiently communicating their environmental activities.

## 8.3.8 The Financial Sector

Constant growth in the investments based on social and economic criteria is registered in the UK. An important multi-stakeholder movement was formed under the ethical investments title. It is important to mentioned the UK Sustainable Investment Forum (UKSIF), which also operates outside the UK. Its members are businesspeople, banks, researchers, and NGOs. The forum informs investors on the sustainability criteria when investments are made and also develops the appropriate instruments for the purpose, such as the FTSE sustainability indicator. Moreover, UKSIF organizes two or three international conferences annually on issues connected to sustainable development CSR. The regulations for pensions' transparency have been approved in July 2000 in order to raise the level of transparency in the pension funds sector. These regulations are complementary to the already existing Pension Act by the request made to pension funds to take into consideration the social, environmental, and ethical aspects in their investment strategies. This has resulted in the fact that from now on pension funds ask for more information from the companies which appear in their investment strategies. A consequence of this change has been that more and more companies voluntarily published information regarding their social and environmental activities.

## 8.3.9 Public Procurement

In general, the connection between public contracts and their compliance with the accepted environmental standards, society, and human rights is still small. Government is trying to orient public procurements, a roughly £13 million annually, toward adopting criteria for sustainable development. Moreover, since 2003 all contracts with the ministries must be in compliance with a specific minimum in environmental standards. Created in 2005, the Work Group for Sustainable Procurements had to elaborate a proposal until April 2006 which contained the transformation methods of the British public procurement system into one of the most sustainable systems on the continent.

## 8.3.10 Business Activities Outside Great Britain

DPDI collaborates with ETI. The initiative is considered to represent a multi-stakeholder successful platform for companies, unions, and NGOs also outside the frontiers of the UK. The main purpose of this initiative is that of improving work condition and the added value in the textile industry business chain. Up to now, 36 companies have received their titles of ETI member, thus committing to offer useful guidelines in their collaboration with suppliers. In 2002, at the World Sustainable Development Summit in Johannesburg, PM Tony Blair published the Extractive Industry Transparency Initiative. The purpose of this initiative is raising transparency within companies from the primary materials' sector, regarding their turnovers and payments, to the governments. The initiative was especially focused on states that are rich in natural resources and the companies doing business there. Approximately, 20 states are members of the initiative or are implementing the EITI principles. The implementation is based on the EITI Source Book, which contains indications regarding the correct applications of the principles.

# 8.4 Case Study: France

Country profile: France
Full name: The Republic of France
Capital: Paris
Population: 62.6 million
Surface: 543,965 km$^2$
Official language: French
Official religion: Christianity
Life expectancy: 78 years (men), 85 years (women)
Official currency: Euro

Main exported goods: machines, agricultural products
GDP per capita: US $42,390

### 8.4.1 The Understanding of CSR in France

Historically speaking, the subject regarding sustainable development in France has been strongly influenced by social considerations. Examples confirming this include the public–private partnership in fighting against discrimination (Fonds d'Action et de Soutien pour l'Intégration et la Lutte contre les Discriminations—FASILD), an organization which promotes integrity and combats discrimination. Made long before CSR appeared on the national agenda, the Bila social report in 1997 is generally considered the predecessor of present analyses regarding corporate activity and sustainability. The study evaluates approximately 6000 companies with a minimum of 7000 employees. What was specific for France, the efforts included a dialogue between unions and employees. Since then, the variety of debates on issues concerning sustainable development has increased to become among the most thorough in Europe. Social issues continue to arise in all activity areas and have increased due to environmental considerations. For instance, in 2002 the French Environment Ministry was renamed as the Ministry of Ecology and Sustainable Development. The government took a series of measures in recent years in order to promote CSR, among which we count launching initiatives, implementing reforms, and establishing commissions. At the same time, it is still unclear whether organizations integrated elements of CSR in their management strategies or if they are merely meeting the legal criteria in order to work. Some observers feel that the managers of French corporations are merely obeying the law and prefer rather getting fined than including CSR activities in their business strategies.

### 8.4.2 The National Strategy

In June 2003, the French government made the first step in consolidating the CSR initiatives and public policies and, since then, unlike in other states, the National Plan for Sustainable Development refers directly to issues concerning CSR. The strategy has three main objectives: one, developing a national system of reference information; secondly, generating an analysis of the positive and negative examples; thirdly, continuing the development of new socially responsible financial instruments. These activities focus on environment protection. The strategy covers a variety of subjects and tasks, including promoting a more efficient public administration, concerned with preserving resources; implementing reforms in the public sector as well as at a regional and national level; creating a sustainable and uniform financial public policy (*La loi organique sur les lois des finances*) and rearranging public procurement procedures in order to have better sustainable development, especially in the area of environment protection. Through these, the government sets some quantitative objectives for the companies (i.e., reducing greenhouse emissions in the transport sector, or increasing the renewable energy percentage). The second Grenelle law (2010) offers more details and implements France's objectives concerning sustainable development, established in 2009 by the first Grenelle law. This requests private companies with more than 500 employees in the urban area and those with more than 250 employees in the rural area to evaluate their greenhouse gas emissions quantity. The evaluations were made until December 31st, 2012, and need to be updated every three years.

### 8.4.3 Visibility

The observers firmly state that succeeding in having companies aim to raise awareness hasn't been of as high importance in French politics as needed, and the legislation rarely provides an incisive from for public relations. In the CSR area, France is much behind other states, although it has made some progress in the past years. The French government claimed that CSR represents one of the main subjects to be discussed during their G8 presidency in 2003. The final G8 statement regarding encouraging growth and promoting a responsible market economy had the purpose of encouraging companies to implement the CSR standards and be part of a partnership concerning CSR. At the 2006 G8 summit in Europe, France, and Germany and other states returned to discussing promoting human rights and the main employing norms of the International Labor Organization. At the beginning of 2004, the French government established the Friends of the Global Pact Forum, a national business organizations network whose members signed the UN Global Compact commitment regarding responsible business and are committed to promoting and expanding CSR practices. The forum now has 400 members and is ranked as being the largest global association of companies to have signed the UN Global Compact agreement. The network is financially supported by the organization Enterprises for the Environment. An inter-ministerial committee for coordinating CSR was established. It is run by the *Commissaire National du Développement Durable*, and through this France found a useful mechanism of introducing the GLOBAL Compact principles in the national CSR policies. Participants agree that this forum represents an important step in raising awareness regarding CSR among French business managers.

### 8.4.4 Transparency and Reporting

In May 2001, France approved the law concerning the new economic relations, which requires publicly traded companies to publish an annual report on the social and environmental consequences resulting from their economic activities—France became the first state in the world to have this initiative. The report must also mention in what way the company is trying to find solutions regarding these consequences. The law was updated in 2002 with 40 qualitative and quantitative factors. These indicators are various and comprehensive, starting from work standards, training services and issues concerning local administration up to water consumption and other natural resources. In July 2010, France introduced a new reference system (BP X 30-025) regarding good practices for the transparency of information provided by companies regarding the social conditions in the subcontracted distribution chain. The system is currently in an elaboration phase and it is expected that, once finalized, will improve the traceability of products.

### 8.4.5 Criticisms for the System's Efficiency in General

In what concerns legal obligations, France is certainly superior to other European states. However, there are also criticisms regarding the efforts up to this present moment. On the one hand, the methods of verifying the companies' responsibility haven't been specified and, due to the fact that companies have the freedom of choosing the methods they prefer, transparency is limited. The way in which legal criteria are followed in reality is unsatisfactory, and companies' willingness to cooperate is limited. Indicators are another issue. Many feel that these are too general and have a limited applicability for some industries. Moreover, no sanctions have been defined until the present. The ministries for environment, social affairs and the economy cooperate in order to improve this situation and find solutions. Still, the external experts state that the legal obligations have not led to the internalization of the CSR concept in French companies.

### 8.4.6 The Financial Sector

The second Grenelle law, of 2010, requires investment companies and financial management companies in France to act transparently in relation with their investment policy. In July 2010, the French government requested these companies to provide information regarding the way in which they are integrating sustainable objectives in their investment decisions. Moreover, under the 2008 law for modernizing the French economy, the saving plans of corporations are guided toward the idea of sustainability. The law offers employees the opportunity to invest some of their titles in their corporation's saving plan into the common investment fund, the Solidary Enterprise, which was designed within this law.

### 8.4.7 Public Procurement

The national French Action Plan for Sustainable Public Procurement was launched in 2007 and revised in 2010. The main objective of this voluntary plan is to offer a structure for the public policy concerning Sustainable Public Procurement with the purpose of raising awareness among public buyers and provide, at the same time, the necessary instruments for creating a sustainable public procurements process. The Action plan has as purpose ranking France among the first SPP EU states. This also includes the updated objectives of the National Sustainability Strategy of 2003, concerning buildings, energy efficiency, heat, paper and cars and also resumes methods for monitoring the public procurement process. Furthermore, in December 2008, the *Exemplary State* objectives were broadcast on behalf of the PM to all ministers and requested every institution to develop an environment management plan (SPP, waste management, energy management, mobility management, etc.) and to offer proof regarding each ministry's contribution. These directives at the same time establish specific SPP objectives for 20 priority product groups, including IT, energy, paper, automobiles, light, food, and textiles.

### 8.4.8 The Activities of Companies Outside France's Borders

When it comes to sustainability, responsibility for international actions is not regarded as a CSR issue in France, but more as an aspect of development governmental policies—unlike in Sweden, for instance. Still, progress is being made in the CSR area. Companies which wish to apply for public credit or insurance are informed by the French Insurance for Exterior Trade campaign, the French insurance company for external trade, OECD standards for multinational enterprises, and these companies must be aware of the standards. COFACE actually surpasses the OECD provisions in that it includes the protection of indigenous people as one of the standards. The Committee for Standardizing Equitable Trade of the French Regulation Association, the French organization for legal norms, brings together stakeholders in order to develop a system of indicators for equitable trade. Moreover, the Foreign Affairs Ministry provided the necessary resources to create the Priority Solidarity Fund in order to raise the market share of organizations that respect equitable trade. The French Agency for Development, the governmental agency responsible for assistance in development, have defined in 2009 in their portfolio a strategy for controlling social and environmental risks. This has as an objective improving the quality of operations the agency provides concerning social and environmental aspects. FAD uses 32 indicators. An FAD unity was created for implementing this public policy and offering support in projects to protect managers as well. This public policy is applied depending on the projects, directly financed from the funds, or through projects financed by third parties.

## 8.5 Solutions for Implementing CSR Strategies

### 8.5.1 Conduct Codes for CSR

A conduct code for companies can be seen as the main instrument for integrating ethics within organizations. The conduct code states the rights, duties, and responsibilities of companies for its stakeholders. It contains conduct principles and rules, thus enriching decision-making processes and orientation on corporate activities. The conduct code expresses *the ideal social contract* between the company and its stakeholders, which puts into practice, through its principles and conduct rules, the ethical criteria for balancing the expectations and interests of stakeholders. In this respect, the conduct code is also a governing instrument for the relationship between company and its stakeholders, but also a strategic management instrument which provides companies with guidelines in the decision-making process. Moreover, the conduct code offers external stakeholders reference parameters with the help of which they may form their opinion regarding the company's reputation.

An important aspect of a conduct code is the initial elaboration method. A recent study of the implementation of these conduct codes in companies reveals the fact that *at the moment where the organization's members can establish a connection between the provisions of the code and the personal value system, they will be more prone to conform with the requirements of the code and take on a higher commitment for the company*. This shows the importance of an inclusive process in elaborating the ethical code of the company, thus ensuring the fact that the ones responsible for implementing it, the employees, do not feel this norms and ethical practices as forced upon them, but that they are built in accordance with them.

### 8.5.2 Suggestion of Models for the Corporate Conduct Codes

The CSR consulting group *Business for Social Responsibility* (BSR) offers a useful summary of an efficient format for conduct codes for companies:

- A letter of introduction on behalf of the management team or the CEO which sets the attitude of the document from the top, in which the importance of ethics and of the compliance of each employee and of the company are defined
- Statements of mission, values, vision, and guidelines, which reflect the company's commitment to ethics, integrity, and quality
- An ethical decision framework with the purpose of offering employees support in making choices. For instance, a code can ask employees to answer a few questions which will guide them in making ethical decisions in an action plan. The purpose is for employees to think before taking actions and ask for advice when they are not certain. They have to be encouraged to think about this question in the context of an ethical dilemma: *Would you refuse or would you be ashamed to tell your family, friends, coworkers about it?*

8.5 Solutions for Implementing CSR Strategies                    95

- A list of available resources for obtaining advice/guidance and reporting on a misconduct (unethical act)
  - Methods of reporting issues under the protection of anonymity (a helpline)
  - How to contact the officer of the ethics and compliance office
  - A clear definition of the stages of reporting to management
- A list of supplementary resources concerning ethics and compliance and/or identifying public policies and auxiliary procedures and their location
- Applying and implementing mechanisms which address the notion of responsibility and discipline for unethical behavior. For instance, unethical conduct will be the object of disciplinary actions up to the and including the termination of contract.

### 8.5.3 The Content of Conduct Codes for CSR

First, a conduct code for companies must reflect the objectives and values within the company. A conduct code must show how a company wishes to guide its economic activities, taking into consideration their impact upon the stakeholders. In this matter, in choosing the content of the conduct code, a company must take into consideration two processes of creating CSR public policies:

(i) **Identifying stakeholders**: *a process through which the agents (local community, environment, employees, etc.) influenced by the company's activity are identified and thus the responsibility limits of a company are better defined.* There is plenty of specialized literature to help companies in identifying relevant stakeholders. The principle was first developed by R. Edward Freeman in his book *Strategic Management. A Stakeholder Approach*, which gained international recognition and was incorporated in the CSR directives and standards worldwide. The essential question for any stakeholder analysis is: *What kind of agents does the company impact?* This process involves examining the entire activity chain of the company, from management to consumer, including all intermediary steps, in order to identify the impact of each element of the economic activity upon the stakeholders. Examples of the most common stakeholders are usually the shareholders, the employees and the local communities, but the future generations of unknown people in parts of the world susceptible to climate change can also be included.

Only by having a thorough analysis of the processes of the organization and by using techniques such as *Life Cycle Analysis (LCA)* or *Positional Analysis* an exhaustive category of stakeholders can be determined. Once identified, stakeholders must be prioritized, and their interests evaluated depending on the shared value which may be created for each party, bringing benefits to both sides.

(ii) **Dialogue with stakeholders**: *a process through which the interests of the identified stakeholders are accessed in terms of economic activity and appropriate considerations are made in order to reduce the negative impact of* *these parts.* Stakeholders' effective management can lead to a convergence of values along sectors and to lead many business strategists to believe that a shared value becomes the norm in what concerns economic activities. Also, there is an important number of forums founded in order to facilitate communication between stakeholders and can be used by companies in creating a conduct code. Such approaches depend on the type of company and can vary from traditional relational tactics to using social media channels. Petra Kuenkel, on behalf of the Collective Leadership Institute, named several common traits of stakeholders' strategic commitment; this is their summary:

- *Challenges based on facts (issues) for each participant*
- *Targeted activities preventing difficulties and which isn't merely a reaction to already emerging problems*
- *It is measurable in what concerns the values and internal purposes of a company*
- *It is based on a meticulous methodology, understood by every party*

### 8.5.4 Implementing Conduct Codes

A good conduct code is characterized by the presence of implementing mechanisms associated with it. These include activities the organizations must do (or revise) in order to support the spreading and understanding of the code's provisions, in order to raise awareness of the shared values and conduct rules, but also to monitor an effective implementation of the code and to administer periodical evaluations. These activities are, for instance, the following:

- *Introducing training activities on ethics-related subjects*
- *Naming an ethics and compliance officer*
- *Creating an advisory board with the task of supervising but also making decisions, i.e., for sanctions*
- *Creating a whistle-blowing mechanism (useful for both employees and eternal stakeholders in order to warn or report unethical activities)*
- *Creating an ethical audit position extends financial management and audit activities and helps to verify the ethical nature of the company's behavior and its procedures*
- *Developing corporate reporting activities (responsible accountancy, social and ethical responsibility, reporting sustainability, etc.), with the help of which the organization communicates periodically the degree of social, environmental and economic impact of its activities on the external environment, and also evaluates the obtained results in relation to its commitments under the conduct code.*

## 8.5.5 Monitoring Progress

As mentioned above, one of the most useful compliance monitoring methods with the help of conduct codes has the form of an annual Communication of Progress, which is emitted voluntarily by companies as part of the UN Global Compact commitment, a universal agreement accepted for ethics in the business environment. These reports not only serve as a standard for the progress of implementing the conduct codes, but also act as a method of external communication through which the stakeholders are informed of the commitments of the organization to the principles of Global Compact and to the personal conduct code. While the general format of COP is flexible, each COP must contain the following three elements:

- *A communication from the CEO through which he/she expresses support for the Global Compact principles and through which the continuous commitment to the initiative and its principles is renewed;*
- *A description of practical actions (more precisely reporting any policies, procedures, and relevant activities) which the company will have to take into consideration in each of the four areas (human rights, work, environment, anticorruption);*
- *A method of measuring immediate results (more precisely the degree to which the indicators/performance objectives or other methods of measuring results were attained/accomplished).*

COPs are made public on the Global Compact's webpage when they are published by the participant. Moreover, Global Compact shares the COP information with the financial markets with the help of Bloomberg LP (a private capital company for financial software, data and media with its headquarters in New York). Public access to the information from the COP promotes transparency, allowing stakeholders to make sure the organization respect their commitment to the Global Compact principles. Also, this offers stakeholders important information which helps them make decisions related to the companies they interact with, as consumers, investors, or employees.

## 8.5.6 Responsible Accounting for Society and Environment

The most efficient method of monitoring progress in implementing the conduct code in the business strategy for companies which do not enter the Global Compact group is Social and Environmental Accounting (SEA). It is an extension of the traditional accounting procedure which, unlike the traditional one, takes into consideration, besides the financial aspects, the company's influence on society and the environment it operates in. This aspect observes the concept of *triple bottom line*, discussed in the introductive part of the document.

Social accounting is the main method through which industries keep their CSR position credibility and thus encourage consumer trust, on the one hand, and their business integrity, on the other one. By raising the level of transparency of the activities of the company, relevant stakeholders are more easily identified and it is easier to create clear communication lines, thus improving CSR's functionality. In a European context, social accountability for large companies is compulsory by law,[5] as it is stipulated that the annual publishing of *detailed information related to employees and environmental issues is necessary in order to understand the company's level of development, but also its market performance*. Besides this provision, many member states applied a stricter legislation when it came to releasing public information, some of which cases will be analyzed in detail in the following sections.

By voluntarily releasing information of a public character related to CSR activities, not only did companies benefit from legislative compliance, but also from the competitive advantage this value creates. As mentioned above, GRI establishes standards for social reporting, the most up-to-date directives being the G4 directives published at the beginning of 2013. These have been presented in two parts:

- *The first part*—**reporting principles and information divulging standards**—presented principles of reporting, information divulging standards and the necessary criteria to be applied by organizations and prepared their sustainability report respecting the directives
- *The second part*—**the implementation manual**—contained explanations related to how to apply the reporting principles, how to prepare the information which will be divulged and how to interpret various concepts of the directives.

To summarize, the first part has directives on *how* to report on time and the second one offers guidelines on *what* to report. Following these guidelines offers companies the possibility of watching the implementation process of the conduct code and of the CSR policy in general, while at the same time improving the transparency of economic activities.

---

[5]Directive 2003/51/EC of the European Parliament and of the Council amending Directives 78/660/EEC, 83/349/EEC, 86/635/EEC and 91/674/EEC on the Annual and Consolidated Accounts of Certain Types of Companies, Banks and Other Financial Institutions and Insurance Undertakings.

# Chapter 9
# Models of Good Practices

Călin D. Lupiţu and Adrian F. Cioară

The selected companies are considered leaders in their work field, having high-rank business strategies, every one of them being in the top 100 of the Global Fortune 500 of the richest companies in the world. These companies have been chosen because they come from different industries, but also for their reputation as pioneers in integrating CSR in the traditional business models.

## 9.1 Case Study: Anglo-American PLC

Anglo-American PLC is a multinational mining company with headquarters in London, Great Britain. It is the largest platinum producer in the world, with approximately 40 % of the global capacity, and an important producer of diamond, copper, nickel, iron ore, metallurgical coal, and thermal coal. This company is active in Africa, Asia, Australia, Europe, North America, and South America. Anglo-American has a primary listing on the stock exchange (appears to be listed first at the London Stock Exchange, the primary market where a company's assets are traded) at the London Stock exchange and is part of the FTSE 100 Index (it is an indicator of the stocks of the first 100 publicly traded companies at the London Stock exchange with the biggest market capitalization). The company had a market capitalization of approximately £31.2 billion as of December 23, 2011,

---

C.D. Lupiţu (✉)
Emanuel University of Oradea, Oradea, Romania
e-mail: calin.lupitu@emanuel.ro

A.F. Cioară
Griffiths School of Management, Emanuel University of Oradea, Oradea, Romania
e-mail: adrian.cioara@emanuel.ro

© The Author(s) 2016
S. Văduva et al., *Integrity in the Business Panorama*,
SpringerBriefs in Business, DOI 10.1007/978-3-319-33843-9_9

becoming the 15th largest company of those with a primary listing at the London Stock Exchange. The second listing is at the Johannesburg Stock Exchange.

### 9.1.1 CSR Vision

> *I think we must fulfill our role, next to our stakeholders, in order to comprise a new informal definition of the concept of social compact for companies.* — Sir John Parker, Anglo-American Chairperson, 2012.

The most recent sustainability report of the organization followed the idea of long-term strategic development. As a mining company, Anglo-American feels that an important argument which ensures their right of mining comes from the local community where they develop their activity and that is why the principles which ensure their shared value for stakeholders and the company are vital in their profit-oriented strategy. CSR, in their vision, represents an essential part of increasing the company's value in general. *Without a sustainable and healthy company we cannot make sure the value is extracted from the mining activities and shared between the stakeholders.* A good citizenship policy permeates the basic business principles and is reflected in the operations performed in all work areas.

### 9.1.2 Strategic Orientation

The general long-term purpose of Anglo-American PLC is that of becoming *world leader in the mining industry, but also the number one investment, favorite partner and employer*. In order to achieve the sustainability objectives their CSR vision has, the company has identified four strategic elements which were incorporated in their business model from the stage of exploiting deposits, through the extraction stage up until the final product. These four elements are summarized below:

- Investments in world-class assets and in those products which, in their vision, deliver the best immediate results through their economic cycle and on the long term—meaning, iron ore, metallurgical coal, thermal coal, copper, nickel, platinum, and diamonds;
- Efficient and effective planning in order to overcome competition throughout the value chain;
- Operating in safety in a sustainable and responsible way, not only because it is fundamental in order to function legally, but also because this way of acting is an important source of competitive advantage;
- Hiring the best people. Anglo-American PLC acknowledges that essential in fulfilling its strategic objectives is to attract, develop, and retain valuable and talented people.

## 9.1.3 CSR Initiatives

As a signing member of the UN Global Compact, Anglo-American PLC has annual evaluations of its registered progress, implementing the ten Global Compact principles. These evaluations offer a useful summary of the most relevant actions performed by a company in the CSR idea. A summary of the most recent evaluations is offered below:

#### 9.1.3.1 Human Rights

The social strategy of Anglo-American was praised in the business environment. The *Anglo-American Social Way* initiative of the company, launched in 2009, summarizes the company's commitments to excel in social performance. A central part of this initiative is the SEAT program (Socio-Economic Assessment Toolbox) which represents the main method through which the company wants to improve the immediate results of the development and capacity of the communities they operate in. Even though social-economic development activities of the company's operations are dictated by local needs, these naturally involve the company's development, responsible investment, and the development of its capacity. Anglo-American PLC has been a signing member of the *Voluntary Principles on Security and Human Rights* since January 2005 and it is a member of the work groups for assistance for governments and also a member in the work group concerning the work area of the secretariat, thus contributing actively to the debates concerning VPSHR activities and, moreover, popularizing their values in states which have not yet adhered to these principles. In 2010, the company was acknowledged by the Institute for Human Rights and Business as one of the first multinational companies to implement a mechanism for complaints, which respects the recommendations of Professor John Ruggle, the special representative for Human Rights and Business of the General UN Secretary. This standardized procedure for complaints and reclamations was introduced in 2010 and it is now compulsory for all company's operations.

#### 9.1.3.2 Work Rights

The Human Resources policy of the group acknowledges employees' rights of association and collective negotiation. Approximately, 70 % of the company's permanent employees are represented in the work council, in unions or other similar institutions and are insured through the collective work contracts. The development code of the supply chain of the company prohibits children's exploitation and includes provisions that the company shall not tolerate forced work, slavery or compulsory prison work. In 2011, the company received the highest marks in the evaluation regarding the way in which the largest companies face children's exploitation risks. The evaluation—led by NBIM, the manager of the Norwegian State Pensions Fund—has offered ten points out of ten to the company for the reporting methods on children's exploitation risk and violation of children's rights in its operations and in its supply chain. Approximately, 50 % of the companies which participated in the survey received zero points. Diversity is very important in South Africa, which is the area with the most employees of the company, and it continues to progress in transforming the demographic elements in the workplace. At the beginning of 2012, Anglo-American became a signer of the *UN Women's Empowerment Principles* in order to contribute to the already made efforts in what concerns improving chance equality between men and women. Women currently represent 15 % of its global work force, an indicator which grew from 10.6 % in 2007 and they occupy 22 % of management positions, an indicator which grew from 15.3 % in 2007.

### 9.1.3.3 The Environment

The precautionary approach of Anglo-American in what concerns environment issues is incorporated in Anglo-American's Environmental Management System and in their *Social and Environmental Impact Assessment,* which is intrinsic for the other eight performance standards which cover key management areas (water, air quality, biodiversity, rehabilitation, mineral residues, nonmineral waste, dangerous substances, and mine closing). The purpose of the SEIA standard is to make sure all Anglo-American projects take into consideration community- and environment-related issues in their planning and decisional processes.

New technology is important in the Anglo-American approach on climate change, an approach supported by a large number of strategic interventions. These pay greater attention to energy efficiency through projects which have as purpose reducing carbon level, and through technologies for reducing the carbon footprint and adapting to climate change. At the core of each of the interventions stated above lie innovation, development, and implementation of the latest technologies. Notable examples include research on clean-coal technology and carbon sequestration. An interesting development in the clean energy area is the *Platinum* business partnership between Altergy, an American company for fuel cells and the Government of the Limpopo province for creating and commercializing platinum-free low-carbon fuels across South Africa.

### 9.1.3.4 Anticorruption

The company's business principles prohibit making donations to any political parties or politicians and obliges employees to act transparently and make sure that such individuals or groups do not look for undeserved advantage when they act or when they deal with civil servants. Evaluating corruption and bribery risks is carried out at every department of the company's level using an instrument of evaluating risks developed within the company. Where the residual risk is unacceptably high, actions designed to strengthen environment control will be taken. These include training sessions for employees which take part in high-risk jobs. By the end of 2011, with over 2000 employees, including heads of the company's departments, attended over 130 training sessions in 17 countries. All employees are prohibited from commercializing estate values when they are in possession of confidential information, sensitive to price fluctuation.

The company supports the EITI initiative and annually reports on taxes and royalties made by the company in different countries where they are active. Also, the Speak Up research center of the company, independently administrated, offers secure and confidential methods for employees, contractors, suppliers, business partners, and other stakeholders for reporting on or making known any issues related to conduct contrary to the company's values and standards.

## 9.1.4 Independent Evaluation

The results presented in the company's annual sustainability report are independently assessed by the Price Waterhouse Cooper, Inc. group. The report where the above-mentioned results were obtained was elaborated at the highest degree by the auditing company. Moreover, an impressive number of independent monitoring organisms accredited the CSR performance of the company.

### 9.1.4.1 Business in the Community

It is a charitable UK organization which developed a platform through which organizations can have a positive impact one society. Its members are committed to improving the way in which they manage their resources but also the way in which they share know-how and expertise and develop responsible business practices addressing the needs of the community and of the environment.

The most important UK rank for voluntary corporate responsibility is operated by BITC; it has been evaluating the company's position since 2000. In a recent feedback report, BITC awarded the Platinum status to Anglo-American PLC for the third year in a row, thus acknowledging the company as one with some of the highest performance rates. In 2012, the company was the only mining company which reached the 80 % compliance standard for each of the main criteria of the ranking.

### 9.1.4.2 The Dow Jones Sustainability Index

The Dow Jones sustainability indexes were launched in 1999 and were the first global indexes recording the financial performance of the companies which have sustainable activities worldwide. The cooperation between Dow Jones, STOXX Limited and Sustainable Asset Management offers managers objectives and reliable standards with the help of which they can manage sustainable portfolios. The Anglo-American company is part of DJSI since 2003 and has managed to maintain its position ever since. In 2010, in recognition of the company's performance in relation to key sustainability criteria, the company received the *Gold Class* status in the DJSI sustainability yearbook—only one in three companies managed to obtain this prize at a global level. Only 10 % of the 2500 companies invited to participate in the annual survey are selected to appear in the Index. Evaluation, carried out by an external auditor, covers economic, social, and environmental performances and includes a summary of policies and performances in corporate governance, risk management, climate change, energy consumption, health and safety, distribution chain standards and workplace relationships, among other criteria.

#### 9.1.4.3 The Carbon Disclosure Project

It is an independent nonprofit organization which holds the largest database with first-hand information for corporations, regarding climate change. Organizations contribute to this database by measuring greenhouse emissions and by sending information along with their strategies regarding climate change to CDP. Anglo-American has participated by transmitting information regarding greenhouse emissions and their climate change strategy ever since the CDP project was launched. In the summary published in 2010, the company scored 85 points and the listed subsidiary 89—a top performance in the sector of mining companies.

#### 9.1.4.4 The Global 100 Ranks

Each year, at the Global Economic Forum in Davos, the *Global 100* ranking positions the most successful 100 companies at a global level. This classification was initiated in 2005 by Corporate Knights (a Canadian media, research and investment studies company) and it is perceived as the most trustworthy way of evaluation, having as criteria the information published by companies. In the ranking made in 2013 (based on the 2012 performances), Anglo-American, with its subsidiary Anglo-American Platinum, was ranked 29th worldwide, the highest position of a mining company.

## 9.2 Case Study: Danone S.A.

The Danone group is the French food-producing multinational with its headquarters in Paris. It claims to be a global leader in producing and commercializing fresh dairy products and bottled water. Besides the Danone/Dannon brands for yogurt, the company owns other internationally renowned bottled water brands: Aqua, Volvic, Evian, and Badoit. Approximately, 56 % of the net sales recorded in 2011 came from dairy, 28 % from drinks, and 16 % from biscuits and cereals.

## 9.2.1 CSR Vision

Danone had a long history of social involvement with its roots by the time when its project, *the economic and social duo,* was launched in 1972. This innovative business strategy suggests that social and economic interests should not go against each other, for a company's duty is to find a way to combine these two elements and make the necessary adjustments depending on the context. It is believed that through this vision Danone does not limit the company and does not restrain it inside a *straitjacket of rigid social and environmental obligations,* but offers it the opportunity of adapting to local environments in order to develop the appropriate models for creating both economic and environmental value for the company. This dual project continues to represent the foundation of the company's social and environmental policies, along with its commitment regarding solving environment issues. The company fully integrated this strategy in its economic operations and became a world leader in reporting sustainability and complying with the GRI recommendations for integrated annual reports.

## 9.2.2 Strategic Orientation

As mentioned above, CSR is integrated in the business model of the Danone group; its strategic objectives not only reflect the financial elements of the stocks' price rising and the maximization of profit, but also the social and environmental elements which also contribute to the value of the company. The Danone Fund for Ecosystem was created in 2009, with the idea of improving the economic and social situation of the local actors in the Danone ecosystem (small farmers, suppliers and subcontractors, transport operators, distributors, regions etc.) throughout their value chain. Structured around five action areas, the fund represents the way in which Danone rise the value of their operation through social and environmental development, thus creating new values. The projects have an impact on many levels of the value chain:

- Ensuring **their raw materials** by supporting dairy and fruit sectors (especially by helping small farmers and/or producers);
- Enhancing **consumer perceptions** on the value of the raw materials, through partnerships for sustainable agriculture;
- **Researching services** that the group can offer consumers in the health area through food products: nutrition and health education, services to support autonomy for old people, children's development, and development with specialized agents;
- **Microdistribution**—through testing the models adapted to new geographical circumstances and populations, in order to address specific issues related to accessibility and employability.

## 9.2.3 CSR Initiatives

Danone's motto of creating *economic value by creating social value* is vital to their world leader position in food production. In 2012, the company mentioned there are four strategic interest areas in ensuring the development of shared values. These form the central elements of Danone's strategic orientation, and the company refers to them under these big titles:

- **Health**—Danone's origins come from the faith that food products represent the main means through which people build and maintain their health;
- **Nature**—Danone thinks that, through health-promoting actions, it also signals its interest in protecting nature. This commitment toward environment is necessary;
- **For everyone**—Danone thinks that, in order for them achieve their objectives, their products must be available to all people in all life stages, in all parts of the world;
- **People**—Danone is committed to respecting good practices in human resource management and social policies.

The above-mentioned strategic objectives highlight CSR's activities framework Danone has and which will form the basis of the analyses of their initiatives. The following are examples of some CSR activities carried out by the company in 2012. All information used about these programs has been collected directly in its annual sustainability report made by Danone for its shareholders.

(i) **Health**—Danone's objectives of bringing health through its food products to as many people as possible involves producing balanced foods which cover health benefits of a large consumer specter and addresses the special needs of each country where the group is present. Danone's strategy covers a vast area of situations related to socio-economic tendencies but also public health issues both globally and locally. At the same time, food security is a fundamental public health issue. It is also crucial in order to maintain the profitability of the group based on consumer's trust and sustainable development. Danone created a specific *product governance* system in order to ensure the quality and safety of its products. This system was created in order to place consumers at the center of its considerations and to sustainably contribute to the group's performance. In 2012, Danone continued to implement the vision of quality in four interest areas:

- **Food security and risk evaluation**—all Danone products worldwide are in compliance with the international FSSC 22000 standard regarding food security;
- **A solid quality system along the product's life cycle**—this system is based on a set of quality criteria (Danone's Operation Models), which define what needs to be done in order to ensure the safety of the products which are in compliance with Danone's specifications in each stage of the distribution chain;

- **Consumers' trust**—consumers' loyalty is determined by efficient feedback management on the markets where the company transactions its goods/services. Quality systems also take into consideration information obtained from consumers and incorporates it in the process of each stage of a product's life in order to offer appropriate results and satisfaction for consumers;
- **Danone employee development**—in 2012 a reference document which contained advice related to career management in quality and had an orientation toward business was distributed to the HR managers of the company. The consequences of this action were seen in quality training, where half a day was dedicated to HR in order to help employees understand and implement this instrument.

Also, Danone took the commitment of promoting the public health concept through its healthy approaches. In this sense, Danone created the first Danone Institute in 1991. Since then, 18 other institutes were created at global level, continuing a network of independent NGOs, whose mission is to improve society's understanding of the link between food, nutrition and health. The work of these institutes is not profit-oriented, and the scientific quality of the programs is related to the multi-disciplinary scientific council responsibility which brings together the most respected and renowned local experts in medicine, nutrition and human sciences.

(ii) **Nature**—in 2008, Danone voluntarily established its objective of reducing pollution's impact on the environment by 30 % in the 2008–2012 interval wherever the group has direct responsibility. The initial objective was exceeded, the group reaching 35.2 % between 2008 and 2012. In 2012, the total emissions of the group were estimated to around 17 million tons of $CO_2$. Since 2007, the group's sales volume had a constant growth of 35 %, while carbon emissions remained constant in general. Starting with these achievements, Danone wished to also involve other companies in this approach, creating the Livelihood Fund in 2011. This fund, which today includes seven other large companies worldwide, invests in big projects on natural ecosystem restoration. These projects contribute to fighting climate change by solving issues generated by big carbon emission volumes. The purpose is to store seven million carbon tons in the next 20 years for a minimum investment of €30 million. The Livelihood fund already invested in six projects in Africa and Asia and contributed to planting over 100 million trees.

Danone is committed to following a strategy to eliminate the impact of deforestation in its distribution chain and realize an afforestation program by 2020. Danone published its position on *Forest Footprint,* which targets transparent evaluation of the deforestation risks in relation to the direct or indirect merchandise used in the group's businesses and proposes specific public policies by classifying its actions regarding the associated risks and impact priorities. This ambition includes paper or cardboard packages, which would impact forests negatively. The commitment has three clear objectives: reducing paper and cardboard weight for each product's packaging, utilizing recycled fibers and, when it is not possible, to use FSC (*Forest Stewardship Council*) certified fibers.

The impact of Danone's economic actions on biodiversity is related, firstly, to the upstream agriculture (soil and water). In 2012, the Brazilian trademark Villavicencio founded an innovative partnership with the NGO Banco de Bosques and implemented the operation *Leave your footprint,* which invited consumers to participate in creating a new natural reserve. For each bottle bought in a 2-month period, Villavicencio committed to protect a square meter from a park. The initiative included the efforts of raising society awareness regarding the dangers produced by deforestation, but also regarding the importance of biodiversity for the local ecosystem, and had a significant impact: approximately 2200 ha were protected, society participated actively in the project, and the overall public's preference for the Villavicencio brand increased.

(iii) **For everyone**—since 2008, the number of Danone consumers has increased by 50 %, from 600 million to 845 million estimated consumers in 2012. Danone continued its geographic expansion, started 15 years ago, into new regions, so that in 2012 new countries represented 53 % of net sales (compared to 17 % in 1996). In order to develop its potential in the long run, Danone experimented with models on a small scale on new markets in certain Asian and African states, as a response to the economic and socio-demographic development, including the emergence of medium-sized cities (with less than 1 million inhabitants) and of the middle class. In Africa, taking into consideration the experience gathered in the last years in the Maghreb region especially, Danone is developing new markets (Ivory Coast, Cameron, Kenya, etc.) through nutritional offers adapted to local conditions in compliance with the WHO code.

(iv) **People**—Danone sees developing abilities as a necessary condition for professional growth. The purpose is to pass on both knowledge and experience, and all Danone employees must share a culture. Developing abilities and leadership are factors the group is known for, as is developing a way to attract and develop quality resources on a large scale in developing states. A new learning strategy was defined in 2012 in order to offer a long-term foundation for the training abilities of Danone employees. Its purpose is creating the perfect conditions for developing resources in regions known for an accelerated development, but also for employees to learn from different types of situations. The Camp 2.0 project, initiated at the end of 2012, supports learning communities and e-learning platforms. *Danone campus* is an original format for a corporate university combining elements of training, networking and exploring general interest subjects, such as social innovation and social business, which was organized in 2012: 13 campus locations were in Europe (France, Czech Republic, Russia), Asia (China, Malaysia, Indonesia and Japan) and in the Americas (Mexico and Argentina), and 3300 people participated.

In order to improve gender equality, Danone addresses issues related to professional life (internal promotions, paycheck packages, work conditions, etc.), career and individual mentality. Key moments of 2012 include registering a higher percent of women occupying top or executive positions, from 28 % in 2011 to 31 % in 2012.

The *WISE* program, launched in 2004, strengthened Danone's commitment to employee workplace safety for approximately a decade. After approximately eight years of continuous progress (the accident frequency rate generated a drop in work absenteeism rates of approximately 60 % between 2009 and 2011), the rates' frequency remained constant for the first time in 2012, at 2.2. These results illustrate that safety is a continuous challenge, and the efforts must be supervised in certain states which host the dairy production division and the French subsidiaries.

## 9.2.4 Independent Evaluation

The 2012 sustainability report Danone published was independently assured by KPMG, which certified that the information presented was based on facts and products in accordance with the GRI directives regarding sustainability reporting. Below are presented examples of some independent accreditations of Danone's CSR strategies.

### 9.2.4.1 The Dow Jones Sustainability Index

Danone was included in DJSI since its establishing in 1999 and obtained an 83 % score in 2012 (from 81 % in 2011), thus confirming its position among leaders of this classification, which for the agro-food industry consists of a committee of 15 worldwide top companies chosen for the 2012 index. Danone obtained, in each of the three Dow Jones criteria, results which were above average, having the highest grade in the economic sustainability area. For this position, Danone obtained a silver category distinction.

### 9.2.4.2 Carbon Disclosure Rating Project

In 2012, Danone entered the Carbon Disclosure Leadership Index for the first time since the group started participating in the CDP project. CDP offers an evaluation instrument for institutional investors and other stakeholders. In 2012, the index had 51 organizations selected for their published information quality and performance in their actions toward mitigating the effects of climate change. Companies with the best results enter the CDLI. The very good results Danone obtained (97 out of 100) highlighted their internal information management's quality and the understanding of climate change-related issues and also its challenges. The result comes as a reward of the high transparency Danone has in its answers.

#### 9.2.4.3 Access to Nutrition Index Rating

ATNI is a new classification index created at the common initiative of the GAIN (Global Alliance for Improved Nutrition) organization, the Bill & Melinda Gates Trust and Welcome Trust. Every two years, the index evaluates nutrition-related policies and practices, as well as the performance of the biggest food and beverages manufacturing companies. This index's purpose is to encourage these companies to improve their products' nutritional quality as well as facilitate access, in order to responsibly influence consumers' choices and behavior. In the first published ATNI ranking, of March 12, 2013, Danone ranked number one, with a global score of 6.3 out of 10, in a group of global leaders companies (Danone, Unilever and Nestlé). The group also obtained the best results in the accessibility, marketing, and commitment categories.

#### 9.2.4.4 Global 100 Rating

Danone held the 75th position in the Global 100 Rating in 2012 and obtained the biggest score out of the companies which activate in the agro-food industry.

## 9.3 Case Study: Bayer

Bayer is a German company in the chemical and pharmaceutical industry, created in Barmen, Germany in 1863. It is well known for its original aspirin, which they invented in 1897. The company celebrated 150 years of activity on August 2013. In 2013, Bayer AG was reorganized into a holding company. The main economic activities of the company were transformed into self-standing companies, all controlled by Bayer AG. These companies are Bayer CropScience AG; Bayer HealthCare AG; Bayer MetalScience AG; Bayer Chemicals AG; and three stock companies with limited liability: Bayer Technology Services GmbH, Bayer Business Services GmbH, and Bayer Industry Services GmbH & Co. The stock shares of Bayer AG are listed on the Frankfurt stock market and the London stock market.

### 9.3.1 CSR Vision

Bayer sees the commitment to CSR and sustainable development as vital to a successful business strategy, thinking that challenges and the issues the planet and its population face are, in fact, business risks which should be managed. There are three key questions which the foundations of Bayer's CSR strategy try to answer:

- How can Bayer AG facilitate access to medical services for the population, in spite of its growth?
- How can crops be optimized and protected in order to obtain high-quality results even in the current environment conditions, where a major issue is represented by climate change?
- How can energy consumption be reduced and how can the effects of climate change be limited?

These three questions are the starting point of Bayer's mission: *Science for a Better Life*, which has as purpose integrating sustainable businesses and high-quality commercial success.

### 9.3.2 Strategic Orientation

The most important objective of Bayer's sustainability strategy is protecting and developing the success the company registered, creating entrepreneurial values and respecting the social ones at the same time. Bayer has as purpose the development of products which can yield real benefits in the future and are safe both in the production and the sales process. This is the only way of generating sustainable and profitable growth and ensuring the future success of the company. Sustainability, thus, makes sense for the company, also economically speaking. More than that, it does not occupy an isolated position within Bayer, but an important part of the corporate strategy, just as the R&D or HR fields. The emphasis, in the sustainability strategy, is on responsible business practices which reduce business risks and on innovations, which pave the way toward new business opportunities which will generate economic, ecological and social benefits. The great social challenges and market shifts resulting from these are the driving engine behind the successful innovations of Bayer. Sustainability is a precondition for research activities and for the development of new drugs, seeds with enhanced plant traits, biological products, and crop protection chemicals and superior quality materials. Innovative products contribute globally for a sustainable development.

*The sustainability program* launched in 2009 puts the strategy into practice. Reference projects in the sustainable medical services area, in high-quality nutrition and in natural habitat and resource protection became well known and the results obtained by the efforts in realizing them will be analyzed in the following section.

### 9.3.3 CSR Initiatives

In order to generate economic, social, and ecological value for the company, Bayer's employees concentrated on several areas of the sustainable strategy. These areas, listed below, form a basis for their CSR activities and are a useful format with the help of which their CSR initiative can be analyzed:

- Improving medical services' quality at global level
- Facilitating sustainable practices in agriculture and reducing the environment's degradation
- Protecting employees and human rights as well as ensuring stakeholders' social protection.

### 9.3.3.1 Provisions in Providing Medical Services

> *We want people to benefit from medical progress, regardless of their income or location. Ensuring medical services worldwide is not a task which any relief organization, government, company or research institute can solve alone. Only a strong partners' network can make things happen.* (Wolfgang Plischle, head of Bayer HealthCare).

As part of the strategy concerning access to medicine, Bayer is developing commercially viable concepts, based on Bayer's expertise pillars and the company's product portfolio. Below are three key points of its activity:

- Supporting parental planning with partners involved in cooperating for international development;
- Supporting the WHO's efforts in confronting tropical diseases and tuberculosis;
- Programs for facilitating patient access to innovative and expensive drugs/treatments, to which a high percentage of the population does not have access.

Bayer promotes parental planning through its commitment to solving the needs of partner organizations in cooperating for international development. In 2012, Bayer entered a new global initiative for improving the access to contraceptive methods with the form of contraceptive implants. The objective is to offer women in developing countries access to contraceptive implants by setting lower prices. In December 2012, Bayer signed an agreement with the Bill & Melinda Gates foundation in order to reduce prices for the implant approved by WHO by more than half. This offered the possibility for more than 27 million women in poor countries to have access to long-term, secure, efficient, and reversible contraceptive methods for a period of six years.

Besides the access to modern contraceptive methods, education and awareness campaigns are also essential for self-determined parental planning. Sexual education is a key requirement for the long-term improvement of future chances of persons in developing stages. Bayer supports an innovative educational program developed with DSW (*Deutsche Stiftung Weltbevoelkerung*), which has a sustainable effect due to its inclusion in the social environment of students and its developing of a methodological guidebook.

In 2012–2013, pharmaceutical companies including Bayer, together with some governments and global health organizations, initiated the biggest campaign intended to tackle the issue of tropical diseases (in terms of cost efficiency, the campaign can be analyzed depending on its sales growth in those countries). The purpose of the London Declaration on Neglected Tropical Diseases was to control or, as much as possible, eliminate 10 tropical diseases by 2020. The companies' commitment is reflected in their expertise area. Bayer's commitment is concentrated on fighting the Chagas disease. WHO estimates Chagas causes a loss in productivity of $1.2 billion annually. The active ingredient produced by Bayer, nifurtimox, can treat almost 100 % of the Chagas patients if the infection is treated in its incipient stages. In 2012, Bayer significantly strengthened their commitment and doubled their investment in tablets available for free to a million people annually. A new formula, with lower dosage, is currently under development in order to provide precise dosages for patients, especially children. Due to the intensified shared efforts of all partners involved under the guidance of WHO, it can be seen that the main objective for the global initiative, that of eliminating this tropical disease by 2020, is attainable. Bayer is also collaborating with partners of the local health systems and NGOs in order to contribute to solving issues which appear in the medical system through helping programs. In USA, Bayer initiated some programs to relieve kidney cancer, and liver cancer; multiple sclerosis patients also obtain treatment from Bayer. The company offers similar products in China and some other states in South and South-East Asia. Those programs go beyond the idea of offering drugs, and, more than that, in the case of chronic diseases, offer support for patients and their families, as well as for medical personnel, and access to diagnosing services.

### 9.3.3.2 Ecology and Sustainability in Agriculture

As a part which completes a €7 billion investment program for 2011–2016, Bayer CropScience invested €5 billion for R&D alone in order to develop new solutions for the operational departments for the protection (chemical and biological) of crops and seeds. The chemical protection of seeds remains essential in many areas of agriculture, if damage related to diseases or pests could be prevented. Bayer is working on developing products which reduce losses due to crop contamination, but still, crop breeding, cultivation, and protection cannot make certain that healthy and durable products will be on the stores' aisles, because a lot of products will be lost along the value-added chain on their way to the consumer.

*Bayer's Food Chain Partnership* (FCPs) supports all actors involved in the food distribution chain—from farmers to food processors to importers and exporters and sellers. Bayer initiated some 240 FCP projects in more than 30 states, especially in Asia, Latin America, and Africa. Bayer CropScience experts advise farmers in what concerns sustainable cultivation in agriculture—starting from seed selection and the controlled utilization of crop-protecting substances, up to the point of monitoring production. Nevertheless, cooperating with partner organizations is now a successful international business model for all the people involved in the food chain. Small farmers from developing countries and emergent markets all have important benefits from having improved production and marketing structures.

### 9.3.3.3 Social Protection and Labor Rights

Being a socially responsible company, Bayer took a long-term commitment in order to support and defend human rights at different levels. Bayer is a founding member of the UN Global Compact and the global human rights promoting commitments. As a global company, Bayer sees this not just as a simple representation of its social and ethical commitment, but also as a necessity for sustainable business. Their purpose is to protect the reputation of top employers, oriented toward sustainable development, and business partners. In order to raise employee awareness of human rights' importance in Bayer's daily activities, the company developed a variety of information and training activities within the group. Its informing program, introduced in 2008, was integrated into a compulsory training session on human rights in most Bayer locations. Compliance with this system is strictly monitored. If there are signs this system is violated, employees can contact their compliance officer and the specially designed compliance phone line in order to signal issues at any moment, and if it is necessary, this can be done under the protection of anonymity. Bayer supports the union representation of its employees. Work conditions for approximately 53 % of its employees are governed by collective agreements or agreements with the firm. In China, establishing union councils for employees, which started in 1997, continued in 2012. Eleven companies from this country now have elected councils which represent and defend the rights of over 10,000 employees. This means that more than 90 % of Bayer's employees in China are now represented by a local union. Also, in 2012 an employees' council was established at a holding company in Japan.

Bayer is convinced that a diversified employees' structure is a vital element in ensuring the company's competitiveness. This is particularly true for management. Diversity gives the company the possibility of benefiting from the innovative and result oriented abilities which are associated with a high level of cultural variety in an organization. Also, Bayer has this purpose especially in the Asian and Latin American economies which are thriving, where the company wishes to significantly increase the local managers' ratio.

## 9.3.4 Independent Evaluations

As it happened for Anglo-American and Danone, the annual sustainability report is independently verified by certified agents. In this case, it was PwC that certified the 2012 report with the highest accreditation standard. Moreover, the report was also certified by GRI, which ranked it as being in full compliance with their standard. This report is the last of this type, as in a sustainability report independent of the financial performances one; starting with 2013, Bayer promised to publish a report in which the financial and non-financial information of the company will be presented in a singular document. More than that, Bayer's sustainability record was acknowledged by a significant number of independent observers. A selection of their results is presented as following.

### 9.3.4.1 Access to Medicine Index—ATM

This index measures and classifies the degree to which pharmaceutical companies' activities facilitate access to sustainable health and especially access to cheap and efficient medication. The indicator scores in the top 20 of R&D pharmaceutical companies evaluated every two years, the first report of this kind being published in 2008. The evaluation is made by the MSCI American agency.[1] The indicator was published for the third time in 2012. After it reached the 14th position in the previous classification, Bayer was ranked nine in the indicator published in 2012, out of a total of 20 R&D pharmaceutical companies evaluated.

### 9.3.4.2 The Dow Jones Sustainability Index 2012

The Bayer Company has been listed in DJSI Global since its establishment in 1999. The company represents a positive class example in what concerns sustainability. This is demonstrated by the 86-point result, above average, obtained by the company in 2012, thus obtaining a silver medal. The decision to include the company in the DJSI Global and DJSI Europe was determined by the *best in its category* principle, only the companies in their sector are qualified—as it is not enough for these companies only to fulfill the basic economic, ecologic, and social criteria. DJSI Global lists 10 % of the companies from a total of 2500 large and very large companies at a global level (Dow Jones Global Index). The best 20 % companies from the 600 big European organizations qualify for the DJSI Europe.

### 9.3.4.3 The Carbon Disclosure Project

Bayer was included in 2012 in both the Carbon Leadership and Carbon Disclosure Project (CDP) indicators. By reaching optimal performance and transparency results, the group reaffirmed its status as one of the top companies in its sector in what concerns environmental strategies. Bayer was one of the 33 companies at global level to be included in the Carbon Performance Leadership index. Bayer repeated the successful feat of the previous year, managing to be the best company in its sector in the CSL index. The latter lists the first 51 companies with the highest transparency level in climate report. For both indexes, the largest 500 global publicly traded companies (FTSE Global 500 Index) are evaluated by the PwC auditors in the name of the organizer of the CDP index. The companies' reports, which represent the basis of the study, are published on the Internet. Only 16 companies are included in both indexes.

---

[1] "MSCI is a world leader in supplying instruments to support investment decisions for approximately 7500 clients worldwide, from ample pension schemes to boutique hedge funds"— http://www.msci.com/about/ accessed on September 9 2013.

### 9.3.4.4 The Institute for Ecological Economy (IÖW)[2]

In 1994, the ranking done by the IÖW evaluated frequently the way in which the largest 150 German companies report on their social and ecological activities, as well as the challenges they face. Companies' sustainability reports are evaluated on the basis of a complete and complex criteria catalogue. The fields evaluated cover reporting global criteria—such as management and sustainability strategy—along with reports on specific activities undertaken by companies concerning their employees' interests, ecology, and production and responsibility operations in the distribution chain, for instance. After reaching the 12th place in 2009, Bayer's report on sustainable development in 2010 reached the 5th place in the 2011 ranking.

### 9.3.4.5 Rio + 20: UN's Conference Regarding Sustainable Development

A network of experts of the Eco-Commercial Building Program (ECB) administrated by Bayer MaterialScience was awarded within the Earth Summit in Rio de Janeiro as a global model of sustainable buildings. The award was presented by the Global Forum on Human Settlements—GFHS) at a conference which it hosted with the UN. The *Best Practice of Global Green Building* Award was presented for recognizing numerous buildings Bayer owns, built according to the ECB concepts.

The global program established by Bayer MaterialScience in 2009 brings together experts from different disciplines which revolve around sustainable building. The program has more than 50 partners, including companies like ThyssenKrupp, Stiebel Eltron and Philips. The objective is planning and building energy consumption-appropriate and optimized buildings, in compliance with a holistic concept. Bayer's buildings in the US, Germany, Belgium, and Italy are examples on this matter.

## 9.4 Case Study: Santander

Santander Group is a Spanish banking group which has the Santander Bank S.A. at its core and represents the Eurozone's largest bank. It is one of the most powerful banks in the world in terms of market capitalization. Its name comes from the name of the city where it first appeared, Santander, in Cantabria, Spain. The group expanded in the last years through an impressive number of acquisitions, with operations developed in Europe, Latin America, North America and Asia. The name and image of many subsidiaries were changed under the name of Santander.

---

[2]Institut für Ökologische Wirtschaftsforschung.

The group is comprised of more than 186,000 employees, 102 million clients, 14,392 subsidiaries, and 3.26 million shareholders. Banking services for individuals—the main component of Santander's operation—generates 74 % of the group's profit. In April 2013, Santander was ranked 43 on the list of the globally largest companies, a list made by Forbes Global 2000.

### 9.4.1 CSR Vision

> *We are also convinced that sustainability comes from trust and now, more than ever, generating trust is essential for the company—it's a game changer*—Emilio Bontin, CEO.

Santander's CSR vision supports the idea that sustainability starts with one's own business; it is necessary to have a solid business model engaged in generating a stable and repeated income. For Santander, CSR also means:

- Taking into account ethical, social, and environmental criteria in the decisional process;
- Having a long-term vision in the relationship with the stakeholders;
- Contributing to the progress of the communities they are present in and operate in.

Market interest in sustainability is increasing more and more. It is essential for big companies to maintain their positions in the CSR indexes, such as DJSI or FTSE4Good, which also have to become the best corporate sustainability evaluators.

### 9.4.2 Strategic Orientation

For Santander, sustainability involves achieving business targets but at the same time, contributing to the economic and social progress of the communities where it is present, by taking into consideration its impact on the environment while protecting the relationships established with the main stakeholders. This business model, together with a solid corporate governance structure, offered Santander the capacity of maintaining its leader position among other prestigious international banks in a difficult economic time, without getting any help from the State. Sustainability is incorporated in Santander's business model and strategy, as well as in the internal processes and policies. Santander feels that its sustainable position is made through a client-oriented agenda, which can be split into three big areas of activities:

- Corporate governance and risk management, which ensure integrating sustainable practices in the daily activities of the company;
- Sustainable internal activities, which rationalize the business process and cut costs;

- Social investments concentrated on education, financial inclusion and entrepreneurship, which add to the organization's value by improving reputation and through establishing a client base interested in Santander's financial products, which are expanding.

## 9.4.3 CSR Initiatives

The essence of Santander's CSR activities comes from the corporate structure itself. The company feels that only through sustainable business practices can it maintain its control on risk management and reputational risks as well, which are extremely important in ensuring the organization's competitiveness. It is useful to evaluate Santander's CSR initiatives from the perspective of the three categories explained above, related to sustainability within the company.

### 9.4.3.1 Corporate Governance and Risk Management

Santander created a committee comprised from top managers, which supervise integrating sustainability in the business model. For that to happen, the committee defines the projects and policies and submits them for approval to the executive board. The committee is chaired by the CEO and includes the executives of the main subsidiaries and support departments of the bank, such as the Bureau of the General Secretary and Financial and Agro-banking Transactions, HR, Technologies and Operations, Risk, and University Departments. The secretary of the committee is the Director of the Sustainability Department, which is part of the Communication, Corporate Marketing and Research Department. This area is responsible for the management and promoting of sustainability across the whole group and also for coordinating various actions. The secretary of the sustainability committee, along with the position of member of the executive board, has the responsibility of coordinating four sub-committees with different sustainability-related tasks. These committees are the committee for socio-economic risks, the committee for the local environment, the committee for climate change, and the committee for volunteers. Each of these committees sends reports regularly to the sustainability committee regarding their progress in implementing CSR in each of the companies' activities.

Reputational risk is the risk related to the perception of different groups the bank is dealing with in its daily economic activities of the bank itself. The risk committee proposes risk policies to the group and to the board and it is responsible for global risk management. Moreover, the committee evaluates the reputational risks in the operational functions and also the decisional risks. The committee for audit and compliance is responsible, among others, for supervising compliance with the legal norms. It proposes improvements and evaluates compliance with the measures resulted from the reports of the evaluation and consulting and supervision authorities.

### 9.4.3.2 Internal Sustainability

Santander developed in 2012 an energy-saving plan until 2015. The so-called *20–20–15 plan* is much more ambitious than its predecessor and it concentrates on the main ten states the group is present in. The objectives of the plan are to:

- *Reduce energy consumption*: a drop of 20 % was registered in the ten states;
- *Reduce carbon dioxide emissions*: a 20 % drop was registered.

These objectives apply to all subsidiaries of the group, both to small ones and to corporate buildings. In 2012, the group's portal regarding the impact it has on the environment was launched, an initiative whose purpose is informing employees worldwide on the issues the bank has in relation to the environment it operates in. This platform offers information on the policies and international standards the group adheres to, the environment indicators, the progress made regarding reducing the effects of the impact on the environment as well as news related to environment issues. The day the portal was launched it had an impressive number of 19,377 views generated by employees, a record for intranet published news. In Brazil, the bank compensates for its carbon dioxide emissions through the Floresta Santander project (a replantation campaign which up to this moment had a number of 344,700 planted trees, thus compensating for the 68,950 tons of $CO_2$). The project compensates for the carbon dioxide emissions generated by the corporate buildings, subsidiaries, data processing centers, employees' commute but also business travel and supplier activities. The bank also has an online instrument which allows Brazilian employees to calculate individual carbon dioxide emissions. As the core doctrine of sustainable procurements, in the main states where the bank operates, contracted suppliers are required to declare to respect and meet the 10 UN Global Compact principles (the group is a member of the Compact since 2002). In 2012, the group contacted the Deloitte group in order to evaluate the degree of compliance with the Global Compact in its supply chain, concentrating on volume risk and/or its impact on the company.

### 9.4.3.3 Social Investments

Santander contributes to the social and economic development of the communities it operates in through initiatives which promote education, entrepreneurship, financial inclusion, and culture and environment protection. The nucleus of its activity is investing in higher education, as a driving engine for progress. This investment is the result of over 1000 collaboration contracts Santander made with universities worldwide. The bank's investment in universities has reached a total of €130 million in 2012. Santander spent the last 15 years developing a long-term strategic alliance with universities which is unique in the world and differentiates the group from other banks and financial organizations. The company also collaborates with universities in order to create projects intended for the improvement of education, international experience and the students', teachers' and administrators' mobility, research, know-how transfer, and in order to promote entrepreneurial culture.

Santander collaborates with NGOs and other nonprofit organizations. In compliance with the UN Millennium Development Goals, Santander sponsors local initiatives in order to support children's education through initiatives as Bécalos, project in collaboration with the Mexican Banking Association and the Televisa foundation. This project supports 163,874 students and it is one of the most important educational programs in Mexico. 90 out of 100 students can continue their studies every year thanks to this program. Without it, the number would be somewhere around 30 %. These statistics reflect the importance of the program Santander sponsored from its beginning, either through direct donations, or by client support. Santander is carrying out a microcredits program, facilitating access to credits for the most underprivileged sectors of the population, in order to improve social inclusion, the quality of life and of the environment. The bank offers support and counseling for the CEOs of SMEs, such as tailors, mechanics, food store owners and helps them generate profit and transform their lifestyle.

## 9.4.4 Independent Evaluations

The annual sustainability report of Santander is made independently by Delloite and received the highest trust level. Reporting sustainability is also made in compliance with the GRI standards on social and environmental issues reporting. The following present a summary of the company's position in the independent evaluations.

### 9.4.4.1 Dow Jones Sustainability Index

In 2012, Santander was ranked in DJSI for the 12th year in a row and it is one of the first 15 most sustainable financial entities according to this index, out of 200 companies which were analyzed. It obtained a total of 83 points, thus being the highest ranked Spanish bank. The result the group had in the 2012 ranking was improved by four points compared to the one of 2011. The score is a positive signal especially due to the fact that it was obtained thanks to good results in such criteria as management systems, different corporate policies such as fighting corruption, strategies regarding climate change and environment management, good practices for talent development, social action, education, risk management, and brand management.

### 9.4.4.2 Carbon Disclosure Project

Santander has been a signing member of CDP since 2007. CDP is the international standard for companies which report information on climate change. The initiative was supported in 2007 by 655 institutional investors which together administrate assets of over 578 billion.

The bank obtained in the 2012 CDP report a result of 79 points for transparency and grade C for performance. Also, in 2011 Santander became a signing member of Carbon Action and in 2012 signed for CDP Water.

### 9.4.4.3 Business in the Community

Santander's UK subsidiary is a member of BITC since 2001. In 2003, BITC praised Santander's community action project named *Breakthrough Program*, awarding it the *Big Tick* award for positive social action. *Breakthrough* is a foundation which targets SMEs which have a rapid growth through investments and trainings. The ones whose experiment is also called *Growth Champions* are responsible for two-third of the jobs created by SMEs in the UK. This means that, through their support, Santander can have the biggest impact in the economic development and create jobs.

# Conclusions

All businesses have principles and aspirations. High business aspirations are tested by the short-term profit opportunities. Willpower must be untouched by these short-term winnings, in order to place on the long run a healthy business at the principles and actions' level. Businesses have an identity or ethos. Integrity imposes that these defining principles and values of the ethos be aligned with both behavior and actions. Acting in contradiction with one of the defining commitments of the ethos means acting without integrity. Companies can stimulate ethical behaviors in order to create a moral character or culture of integrity. This requires decisions to be made with *supporting the point of view* in a *community of co-regulators*. In the business environment this is translated through the fact that the business has to have social responsibility. Society's attitude must be placed at the center of the decision-making process. Integrity in business requires committing to those aspects in order to lead to unity in character and actions. The values and principles comprised in an ethic code offer ethos the definition of the commitments of the business. Policies and procedures guide the behavior of a set of individuals in order to confer a culture of integrity. The management gives *the tone from the top*. The tone leadership sets is essential in formulating and practicing the business' values and commitments.

Promoting integrity is vital in combating day-to-day illegal and unethical practices which can appear in the business environment. Corruption undermines integrity and, with it, the legitimacy of public and democratic institutions of the state, it weakens the moral values of the society and generates uncertainty in the economic environment. Corruption appears when there are inadequate revisions, and the weak control systems and bad governance offer limited chances of exposure and punishment. Building integrity in the business systems and promoting a culture of integrity are essential in fighting against corruption. Integrity is a natural agent of combating corruption and companies which place it at the center of their activities are less sensitive to corrupt activities. Integrity in business requires more than avoiding corrupt activities. It offers guidance in business situations which involve complex ethical dilemmas. A culture of high-level integrity in a business inspires its moral actions over these daily dilemmas. Building long-term relationships based on trust is fundamental for the future success of the business. *Without trust, business as we know it cannot exist.* Integrity is a fundamental component in building relationships based on trust. A business which has integrity is seen as trustworthy. Thus, the tendency of offering trust to a partner will increase. Trust absorbs uncertainty from the possible business relationships and integrity reduces the risk associated with this uncertainty. Trust in business integrity promotes entrepreneurial spirit and creativity, it ensures the vitality of the market system and it increases society's wealth. The law is, in essence, *an institutionalization or codification of ethics in specific social norms, regulations and interdictions*. Still law and ethics are not identical. The law is a system of the minimum acceptable behavioral standards within a society; thus, respecting it becomes a minimum compulsory standard in building integrity in the business environment. The legal limits which reflect society's principles must be obeyed.

Last but not least, we highlight the fact that society's sensitivity regarding the fundamental principles and values of social justice have increased and businesses must be aware and take into account these trends. Businesses, as a central pillar of society, have the democratic rights of actively discussing the nature of laws, but must also respect them. Laws have the purpose of promoting fairness and consistency and offer, in addition, a solid foundation upon which trust is built.

# Recommendations

Although it is far from representing a treatment for climate change or sustainability crisis, CSR demonstrated the potential of increasing the value of all three dimensions of the *three bottom line* concept and offers significant gains to the population, the planet, and the companies' profits. Based on the results presented in these pages, a series of recommendations were made:

**Recommendations for decisional factors**

- *Developing specific guidelines for each country, based on international standards*
- *Increasing CSR knowledge through campaigns*
- *Increasing CSR information quantity through campaigns*
- *Producing a change through the power of personal example by developing CSR policies for companies with public capital*
- *Encouraging good practices through rewards and economic incentives*

**Recommendations for organizations leaders**

- *Identifying fundamental values and business objectives in order to develop a strategy designed to reach these objectives responsibly*
- *Developing conduct codes in cooperation with stakeholders and offering continuous evaluations*
- *Concentrating on concrete objectives which are easier to be communicated by team members and easier to be implemented*
- *Developing a culture of transparency within the organization by maintaining high standards in what concerns releasing public information*

**Recommendations for community stakeholders**

- *Increasing market pressure on companies so that they act responsibly by including CSR registers in buying preferences*
- *Organizing the independent community in CSR monitoring associations, which evaluate objectively the economic activities of companies, like those from the British* Business in the Community *foundation*

- *Taking up commitments to the business environment in order to build constructive and synergy relationships which create shared values*
- *Engaging modern social media techniques in order to report companies which fail to reach their own CSR standards.*

# References

1. Audi, R., *Some Dimensions of Trust in Business Practices: From Financial and Product Representation to Licensure and Voting*, Journal of Business Ethics 80,no. 1 (2008)
2. Besanko, D. et al., *Economics of Strategy*, Wiley, 2012.
3. Boatright, J.R., *Ethics and the Conduct of Business* (Prentice Hall, 1997).
4. Cheshire Calhoun, "Standing for Something", *The Journal of Philosophy,* Vol. 92, No. 5 (May, 1995), pp. 235-260.
5. Clark, K.B. & Fujimoto, T., *The Power of Product Integrity*. (Cover Story), Harvard Business Review 68, no. 6 (1990).
6. Copeland, N., EP Library briefing: *Review of the European Transparency Register*: http://www.europarl.europa.eu/RegData/bibliotheque/briefing/2013/130538/LDM_bRI(2013)130538_REV1_EN.pd
7. Crane, A. & Matten, D., *Business Ethics: A European Perspective: Managing Corporate Citizenship and Sustainability in the Age of Globalization*, OUP, Oxford, UK, 2010.
8. Cravens, D.W. & Piercy, N., *Strategic Marketing*, McGraw-Hill, 2005.
9. Daryl Koehn, "Integrity as a Business Asset", *Journal of Business Ethics* Vol. 58 No. 1-3 (May 2005), pp. 125-136
10. Das, T. K. & Teng, B., *Between Trust and Control: Developing Confidence in Partner Cooperation in Alliances* Academy of Management Review 23, no. 3 (1998)
11. Dundon, T. et al., *The Meanings and Purpose of Employee Voice* International Journal of Human Resource Management 15, no. 6 (2004).
12. Dyer, J.H., Kale, P., & Singh, H., *How to Make Strategic Alliances Work* (Cover Story), MIT Sloan Management Review 42, no. 4, 2001.
13. Fagan, C. (2009). *What Is a Conflict of Interests?* retrieved from http://blog.transparency.org/2009/07/27/what-is-a-%E2%80%98conflict-of-interest%E2%80%99/
14. Frankel, M.S. *Professional Codes: Why, How and with What Impact?*, Journal of Business Ethics 8, no.2/3 (1989)
15. Gerber, D.J. *Fairness in Competition Law: European and U.S. Experience. Prepared for presentation at a Conference on Fairness and Asian Competition Laws.* (March 5, 2004 Kyoto, Japan)
16. *Gerhold K. Becker,* „Integrity as Moral Ideal and Business Benchmark", *Journal of International Business Ethics Vol. 2 No. 2 (2009).*
17. Gilman, S.C. *Ethics Codes and Codes of Conduct as Tools for Promoting an Ethical and Professional Public Service: Comparative Successes and Lessons*, Washington, D.C., 2005
18. Gorden, W.I., *Range of Employee Voice.* Employee Responsibilities and Rights Journal 1, no. 4 (1988)
19. Hargreaves, S. & Homewood, M.J., *EU Law Concentrate: Law Revision and Study Guide*, OUP Oxford, 2013

© The Author(s) 2016
S. Văduva et al., *Integrity in the Business Panorama*,
SpringerBriefs in Business, DOI 10.1007/978-3-319-33843-9

20. Howard, M.C., *Public Sector Economics for Developing Countries*, University of the West Indies Press, 2001.
21. Kanter, R.M., *Collaborative Advantage: The Art of Alliances*, Harvard Business Review 72, no. 4, 1994.
22. Kaufmann, D., *Six Questions on the Cost of Corruption with World Bank Institute Global Governance Director Daniel Kaufmann*, Washington, D.C.: The World Bank, 2005
23. Keenan, D.J. & Smith, K., *Smith and Keenan's Law for Business* (Pearson Longman, 2006)
24. Krajewski, M., *Legal Framework for a Mandatory EU Lobby Register and Regulations*, 2013.
25. Laszniak, G.R. & Murphy, P.E., *Fostering Ethical Marketing Decisions*, Journal of Business Ethics 10, no. 4, 1991.
26. Leventhal, G.S. *What Should Be Done with Equity Theory?* in Social Exchange, ed. Kenneth J. Gergen, Martin S. Greenberg, and Richard H. Willis (Springer US, 1980).
27. Liden, R.C., Bauer, T.N., & and Erdogan, B., *The Role of Leader-Member Exchange in the Dynamic Relationship between Employer and Employee: Implications for Employee Socialization, Leaders and Organisations* in J. Coyle-Shapiro, L. Shore, S. Taylor, & L. Tetrick (Eds.). The Employment Relationship: Examining Psychological and Contextual Perspectives. (pp. 226-250), (Oxford University Press 2004).
28. Lind, E.A. & Tyler, T.R., *The Social Psychology of Procedural Justice*, Springer, 1988
29. Mayer, R.C., Davis, J.H., & Schoorman, F.D., *An Integrative Model of Organizational Trust*, 1995
30. McGrath, C. *Comparative Lobbying Practices: Washington, Londra, Bruxelles*, paper presented at the annual Political Studies Association conference, Universitaty of Aberdeen, 2002
31. Mungiu-Pippidi, A., *The Good, the Bad and the Ugly: Controlling Corruption in the European Union*, (Hertie School of Governance, 2013)
32. OECD (2005), *Conflicts of Interests in Policies and Practices of 9 EU Member-States: A Comparative Analysis*, Sigma Papers, No. 36, OECD
33. OECD (2010), *Recommendations of the Council on Principles for Transparency and Integrity in Lobbying*
34. Patrick E. Murphy, „Eighty Exemplary Ethics Statements" (Notre Dame University Press, 1998)
35. Perry, C., Cavaye, A., & Coote, L., *Technical and Social Bonds within Business-to-Business Relationships*, Journal of Business & Industrial Marketing 17, no. 1 (2002).
36. Putnam, R.D., *Bowling Alone: The Collapse and Revival of American Community,* Simon & Schuster, 2000
37. Putnam, R.D., Leonardi, R., & Nanetti, R.Y., *Making Democracy Work: Civic Traditions in Modern Italy* (Princeton University Press, 1993)
38. Reed, Q. (2008). *On the Fence: Conflicts of Interests and How They Are Regulated*, U4ISSUE 6 (2008)
39. Seijts, G.H. & Crim, D. *What Engages Employees the Most, or, The Ten C's of Employee Engagement*, Ivery Business Journal 70, no. 4 (2006).
40. Smith, N.C., *Marketing Strategies for the Ethics Era*, Sloan Management Review 36, nr. 4 (1995).
41. Spencer, D.G., *Employee Voice and Employee Retention*, Academy of Management Journal 29, no. 3 (1986)
42. Storey, T., Turner, C., & Martin, J., *Unlocking EU Law*, 3rd ed., Hodder Education, 2011.
43. Stueart, R.D. & Moran, B.B., *Library and Information Center Management,* Libraries Unlimited, Incorporated, 2007.
44. Sztompka, P., *Trust: A Sociological Theory*, Cambridge University Press, 1999
45. Transparency International, 2007. *Combating Corruption in Judicial Systems.* Berlin:TI
46. Transparency International, *Money, Politics, Power: Corruption Risks in Europe*, 2012
47. Tyler, K., *Undeserved Promotions: A Researcher Uncovers Evidence of Rampant Favoritism in Promotion Decisions*, Society for Human Resource Management, 2012.
48. World Bank, *Helping States Fight Corruption: The Part Played by the World Bank* (1997)
49. Zak, P.J. & Knack, S., *Trust and Growth,* The Economic Journal 111, no. 470 (2001)

Printed by Printforce, the Netherlands